P9-CFD-038

REAL MEN
PRAY THE ROSARY

"This book is a must for every soldier of Christ! The Blessed Mother tells us that the Rosary is a sword that cuts through evil. It is a prayer that carries with it a powerful and mysteriously effective force that should never be taken for granted. *Real Men Pray the Rosary* is a great help in emphasizing this important truth! We are all on this battlefield together, and each one of us plays a critical role in the world to do what our Lord commissions us to do. Through the Rosary, we are trained and strengthened to do the work that God calls us to do. I encourage all to read and take to heart this great book."

Doug Barry
Cohost of EWTN's *Life on the Rock*

"What could a book written for men tell women? Plenty! I wanted to dash for my Rosary when I finished reading David Calvillo's book, *Real Men Pray the Rosary*—a testimony that not only do 'Real Men' pray the Rosary, but so do real women! Packed with stories of men whose lives have been deeply influenced by the power of the Rosary, Calvillo's own personal witness, the history of the Rosary, and insightful meditations to aid us in this efficacious prayer, Calvillo has given us a gem of a book."

Johnnette S. Benkovic
Founder of Women of Grace®
Host of EWTN's *Women of Grace* and *Women of Grace Live*

"What David Calvillo has done in his wonderful book, *Real Men Pray the Rosary*, is give us a full picture of the meaning of the Rosary, its origin and place in the history of the Church, and many of the inspiring statements of popes and saints who have encouraged the Rosary as 'the most perfect prayer.' He reminds us that through the Rosary, we learn to pray in all main forms of prayer: with our lips in the words we recite, with our minds as we meditate on the Mysteries, and with our hearts as love grows within us. To illustrate his words about the Rosary, the author has included many testimonies of men whose lives have been profoundly changed by the Rosary. One very interesting feature is the author's use of his tool box with simple exercises to jump-start praying the Rosary. At Fatima, the only request Our Lady made to the shepherd children in all six of her apparitions was to pray the Rosary daily. She told the young visionaries: 'The Rosary is powerful enough to stop wars; the Rosary can bring world peace; the Rosary can convert sinners!' I highly endorse David Calvillo's book, *Real Men Pray the Rosary*. Read it, and you will discover a treasure!"

Andrew Apostoli, C.F.R.
Author of *Fatima for Today*

"For centuries, the Rosary has invited all people to pray, to ponder the treasury of the Gospel mysteries that infuse its beads, and to find a life of purpose as well as peace. David Calvillo shares his own profound and personal walk within these pages. What we find by its end is the beginning of a treasure to share with the world: real men pray, and they pray the Rosary."

Jason Godin
Columnist at Catholic News Agency

REAL MEN
PRAY THE ROSARY
A Practical Guide to a Powerful Prayer

DAVID N. CALVILLO

ave maria press AmP notre dame, indiana

The phrase "Real Men Pray the Rosary," the Rosary in fist symbol, and the RMPTR logo, which consists of a fist holding rosary beads framed within concentric circles, are registered trademarks licensed to Real Men Pray the Rosary, Inc.

Song lyrics of "My Daddy Prayed" reprinted with permission of Michele Galvan.

Nhil Obstat: Reverend Alex Flores, *Censor librorum*

Imprimatur: Most Rev. Daniel E. Flores
Bishop of Brownsville
January 3, 2013

© 2013 by Real Men Pray the Rosary, Inc.

All rights reserved. No part of this book may be used or reproduced in any manner whatsoever, except in the case of reprints in the context of reviews, without written permission from Ave Maria Press®, Inc., P.O. Box 428, Notre Dame, IN 46556, 1-800-282-1865.

Founded in 1865, Ave Maria Press is a ministry of the United States Province of Holy Cross.

www.avemariapress.com

Paperback: ISBN-10 1-59471-376-6, ISBN-13 978-1-59471-376-7

E-book: ISBN-10 1-59471-377-4, ISBN-13 978-1-59471-377-4

Cover image © Ron Chapple Photography/SuperFusion/SuperStock.

Cover and text design by Andy Wagoner.

Printed and bound in the United States of America.

Library of Congress Cataloging-in-Publication Data

Calvillo, David N.

Real men pray the rosary : a practical guide to a powerful prayer / David N. Calvillo.

pages cm

Includes bibliographical references.

ISBN-13: 978-1-59471-376-7 (pbk.)

ISBN-10: 1-59471-376-6 (pbk.)

1. Rosary. 2. Men--Prayers and devotions. 3. Catholic Church--Prayers and devotions. I. Title.

BX2163.C395 2013

242'.74--dc23

2012048379

This work is dedicated to
my parents, Alicia Vera and Joe Calvillo:

Mom, whose love and unceasing prayers bequeathed to me
a love of Our Blessed Mother and of the Rosary, and
Dad, who shows me that a real man prays
and loves his wife

The Rosary provides the Christian with sustenance with which to nourish and strengthen his faith.

—*Pope Leo XIII*

A prayer so easy and yet so rich truly deserves to be rediscovered by the Christian community.

—*Blessed Pope John Paul II*

CONTENTS

FOREWORD

Ever since I became aware of David Calvillo's devotion to the spirituality that is represented by the Rosary—a deeply Marian and very action-oriented spirituality that can be especially appealing and useful for men—I have thought of this prayerful tradition in a different way than I had for so many years.

Upon learning more about the Rosary and putting aside preconceived notions (and frankly even prejudices) about it, I have come to view the age-old devotional practice through a new lens: the lens of my own life as a man in the twenty-first century. The Rosary, viewed through that lens, breaks through the incessant clutter of "information" that all of us face every day. In praying the Rosary, I have thus discovered several of its important attributes.

It is *attractive*. The Rosary draws the attention and devotion of the faithful. Powerfully. Almost irresistibly. The promise of grace and forgiveness of sins draws many to this form of prayer; likewise, the promise of peace, for the individual soul and for the whole world, compels still others to reach for the Rosary with deep passion and longing, hoping to realize these promises in their lives.

It is *active*. The Rosary is an action as well as a give-and-take relationship. It is not merely an inert pile of beads subject to manual manipulation and gravity. Rather, to pray the Rosary requires an act of will and some physical and mental *movement* on the part of the person who participates in this prayer. The Rosary represents an act of seeking a closer relationship—a oneness, in fact—between the believer and the Lord.

It is *creative*. Perhaps this is the most startling component of my new "theory." How in the world could an inanimate object such as a Rosary create anything? That's a silly idea, of course. But the Rosary as a prayer and an instrument of engagement with

God, with the participation of the Blessed Mother—the prayer that is believed to be a gift from God to holy people of previous ages and to our own—can indeed generate spiritual bouquets (how's that for an outmoded notion?), spiritual reflections, and more spiritual and unified families.

I suppose that is all quite a mouthful, but I want to look at the Rosary—and encourage you to look at the Rosary—in a different light. I want to hold it up for a close examination and to look beyond the cliché that it has become for so many people, particularly men. I can do so thanks to David Calvillo's breakthrough, which he describes so eloquently in his personal testimony in the form of this book, *Real Men Pray the Rosary*.

I first came to know of David and Real Men Pray the Rosary, Inc. (RMPTR) when I was reading *The Wall Street Journal* a couple years ago and saw the article that described the apostolate that had sprung up in South Texas thanks to him and his wife, Valerie. I thought, "Gee, I wonder if he has published a book about that." It sounded like a subject that I would enjoy reading about, especially because I am interested in the concept of men's spirituality. The pairing of *men* and the *Rosary* also sounded so unlikely—almost oxymoronic—that I really wanted to know more.

Turns out there was no book, but the idea, when proposed to a friend with connections in the book publishing industry, certainly caught the attention of others. Meanwhile, the message of RMPTR continued to spread and gain momentum through David's own indefatigable energy, along with his wife's involvement and the prayerful support of the group he assembled as a board for his burgeoning organization. Of course, Facebook and other social media helped to spread the word and attract even more enthusiastic followers and friends.

His mother was very ill at the time, and she passed away shortly after I came to know David. That was a powerful, transformative experience for him, which he shares about openly in this book. It was, in a way, a confirmation of the rightness of the path he found himself traveling.

The loss of a mother is hugely traumatic for most people. For men, it can have a devastating effect, whether the son was particularly "close" to his mom or not. I think this is because our moms are the ones who physically bore us and from whom we issued forth, having been created in the image of God, the Father and Creator. We had to come from somewhere (with a little help from our dads, of course), and that *somewhere* is mother.

How poignant it is for all of us to witness Mary, the Virgin Mother of Jesus of Nazareth, standing before the cross on which her son was tortured to death. She stayed with him through all the years of his life and was reunited with him after her own life had ended. The Catholic Church recognizes her with the title *Theotokos*, meaning God-Bearer, and teaches that she—and only she—is now united with him, bodily present, in heaven, before the throne of God. Now that's a powerful mother-son relationship. And it's a relationship that each of us can have with the Blessed Mother through praying the Rosary. For men, David writes, the Rosary can also bring us closer to the other women in our lives: our wives, daughters, sisters, aunts, friends, teachers, and any other women who are important to us. What a gift!

For me, the Rosary has come back into my life over the past several years in subtle yet distinct ways. When I was invited to speak to parish Rosary societies, I made it a point to come early and actually join in praying the Rosary with the women of the societies. On retreats and at various lectures and talks, I kept hearing the Rosary referred to and recommended as a spiritual practice. I found an old Rosary that I had forgotten I owned and that had belonged to my late great-uncle, who had been a Passionist priest. Most importantly, I occasionally picked it up myself to pray in quiet, solitary moments.

Then, with David's suggestion that we turn to the writings of St. Louis de Montfort and the teachings of the popes on the subject, I have since found more of a theological basis for reflection on the prayer and its purpose—and its great promise.

Very recently a dear friend died. He was an elderly gentleman who, for me and many men in our community, represented the epitome of Catholic spirituality and prayerfulness. In addition, he was a pillar of his parish, married sixty-plus years to a woman who had passed away the previous Christmas Eve, a great-grandfather, amazingly fit and active, involved as an alumnus of his Catholic alma mater and with innumerable civic and parish causes. He suffered a brain hemorrhage and lived unconscious for more than ten days as family, friends, and clergy gathered around him.

One of his daughters mentioned in my presence that they didn't have a Rosary and that he had enjoyed praying the Rosary. I brought one from home the next time I visited and had the opportunity to pray it with him. I left it there in his room. At the first visitation at the funeral home, I went up to the casket to pay my respects, and there he lay, with that Rosary entwined in his hands. It was a powerful image that I shall never forget.

Rather than a religious trinket or a corny, outdated Catholic devotion, the Rosary, I have come to learn, is a vital, powerful, attractive, effective means of prayer. Indeed, it is the perfect prayer, as you are bound to discover in the journey you are about to take through this book.

Greg Tobin

ACKNOWLEDGMENTS

With grateful acknowledgment to:

my wonderful wife, Valerie, for her heroic patience as I toiled away at this latest project and for living the Marian virtues that we pray to attain. Living as your husband makes me want to be a better man;

my loving children, David N. II, Victoria D., Joaquin Alejandro, Lazaro Andres, Ana Lourdes, Teresita Alicia, and Maris Stella, for their prayers and for providing the daily vivid reminder of God's abiding presence in my life. Each of you is an amazing blessing;

the priests who pray for me as pastors and friends, Fr. Alfonso Guevara, Fr. Pat Seitz, Msgr. Gustavo Barrera, Fr. Hugh Gillespie, and Msgr. Juan Nicolau. Thank you for your divine vocation and for your prayerful friendship;

Fr. Hugh Gillespie, S.M.M., whose frank and insightful comments made this little work better. Thank you for your continuing visits to "God's country;"

Greg Tobin, my writing "coach," whose guidance and calming influence helped shepherd this project to fruition; and

our Blessed Mother. I lay this little work at your feet that you may present it to your son as a small offering from one of your children. *Ave Maris Stella. Totus Tuus.*

"May the perfect joy of Christ reign in your heart!"

INTRODUCTION

The Rosary is the sweet chain that links us to the events of our salvation. As we travel through her Mysteries, a "gospel in miniature" is presented to us. This gospel, this grace, is given not so that it may be hoarded by us but that we may share it with the world.

I recall my installation as the sixth bishop of the Diocese of Brownsville on February 2, 2010, the Feast of the Presentation of the Child Jesus in the Temple, one of the Joyful Mysteries we pray in the Rosary. On that occasion, I reflected on the Presentation and the Holy Family, which lies at the heart of our devotion to the Blessed Virgin Mary, her spouse, St. Joseph; and her divine son, Jesus Christ.

The Presentation of the Child Jesus in the Temple is a singular moment of joy and communion. Mary and Joseph experience the joyful occasion to return to the Temple in Jerusalem to give thanks to God for the gift of this special child. They understood that the life of the family is not complete unless it is connected to the mystery of the One True God. To attend the Temple was not an obligation binding them to do something they did not really understand. On the contrary, they understood quite well that their family life was a gift from the Father, and they joyfully went to the Temple to fulfill the prescriptions of the Jewish Law. They offered a humble sacrifice of thanksgiving. It was a joy for them because the gratitude was in their hearts even before they make the trip to the Holy City.

It reminds me quite vividly of when I was a little boy, and my mother and grandmother, who prayed the Rosary devoutly, would take us to church to visit the Blessed Sacrament at Holy Hour and light a candle. They took us because they knew very well that the life of the home draws life from its connection with the House of God.

The Presentation is a precious sign of this communion between family life and the mystery of the living God, as well as a moment of communion between the family and the rest of the community.

As Joseph and Mary receive support from Simeon and Anna, we too need support and encouragement from those whose lives have been marked by faith and lived experience. We see the image of the Church reflected in this exchange: a communion of the family with God the Father, with Christ Jesus at the center; and a communion of the whole community of faith with Jesus, Mary, and Joseph happy to be together in the house of the Lord. This is an image we can imitate. Our young families, with their children, seek the grace of heaven in the Church, and they seek the wider community of believers.

I am grateful for the efforts of all those who seek to build up this community of faith here in the Diocese of Brownsville and throughout the Church, as well as lay movements such as Real Men Pray the Rosary and many others that encourage families to pray together.

With that in mind, I would like to personally direct an invitation in particular to the men of our Catholic community. At times we talk among ourselves that the formation of our children, especially in questions of religion or faith, pertain more to our women. Certainly, we have received a powerful formation in the values of our life through the example and teaching of our mothers and grandmothers. Without question, however, my brothers, our children need the example of Christian values from honorable, virtuous men. In addition to the powerful example of St. Joseph, the foster father of Jesus, I commend the Rosary, the prayer of the Mother of God, the Blessed Virgin Mary.

The scriptures don't contain a single word uttered from the lips of St. Joseph. Instead, he speaks through his actions. He dedicated himself completely to the mission of protecting and providing for the Virgin Mary and the child Jesus. His fidelity and justice open the road for Jesus Christ. Christian men, fathers of families, also have a vocation in our times. That vocation is to open the road for justice and for authentic virtues for future generations. If we don't accept that vocation, we risk losing all future generations to violence, revenge, and drugs.

Yes, everyone has a part to play in this sharing in the grace of Christ's love. Men, as fathers and husbands, you are called to love your children, spend time with them, and teach them about what is truly important in life. Likewise, you are called to love your wives without reservation, to stand with them in their work, and to never take for granted the critical role they play in the raising of your children. The women in our lives, our mothers, wives, sisters, daughters, and friends, help us to be the men God intended us to be.

So, let us lift our voices in humble supplication to the Blessed Virgin Mary that she may show us her son and our Savior, Jesus Christ. Let's be men who pray the Rosary.

+ Most Reverend Daniel E. Flores, S.T.D.
Bishop of Brownsville, Texas
October 7, 2012
Memorial of Our Lady of Victory

ENCYCLICALS AND PAPAL DOCUMENTS
ABBREVIATIONS

DAP *Di Altissimo Pregio,* Apostolic Letter of Pope Benedict XV, 1915.

DT *Diuturni Temporis.* Encyclical Letter of Pope Leo XIII, 1898.

IM *Ingravescentibus malis.* Encyclical Letter of Pope Pius XI, 1937.

JS *Jucunda Semper* (on Mary Mediatrix). Encyclical Letter of Pope Leo XIII, 1894.

MDM *Magnae Dei Matris.* Encyclical Letter of Pope Leo XIII, 1892.

QP *Quamquam Pluries.* Encyclical Letter of Pope Leo XIII, 1889.

RCR *The Religious Convention and the Rosary.* Apostolic Letter of Pope John XXIII, 1961.

RVM *Rosarium Virginis Mariae* (On the Most Holy Rosary). Apostolic Letter of Pope John Paul II, 2002.

SI *Salutaris Ille.* Apostolic Letter of Pope Leo XIII, 1883.

CHAPTER 1

THE ROSARY FOR OUR TIMES

As the month of October draws near, a month which we have already dedicated to the Virgin Mary under the title of Our Lady of the Rosary, we earnestly exhort the faithful to carry out this religious exercise this year with the greatest faith, piety and diligence possible. We know that a refuge is at hand in the maternal goodness of the Blessed Virgin, and we are sure that we are not placing our hope in her in vain.

—Pope Leo XIII, *QP*, 2

What Is the Rosary?

The Rosary is many things. It is a powerful story that, when often recited, becomes familiar and inspiring—even thrilling—to many. It is a comfort and a habit, a place to which we return and from which we step out of the world. The Rosary is an object of sacred art, a tactile experience in many media: wood, metal, stone, precious gems, string, and even plastic. But most of all, the Rosary is a prayer; indeed, it is *the* prayer for millions around the world who seek the profound spiritual experience that it promises.

Further, it is a prayer for all Christians—not just Catholics. While throughout this book, I emphasize my experiences and the sources of my understanding about the Rosary, which are primarily Catholic, this book is for all my Christian brothers and sisters, to allow you to take a close look at what this special prayer offers our faith lives.

His Holiness Blessed Pope John Paul II often preached and taught about the Rosary. "The Rosary is my favorite prayer," he confessed. "A marvelous prayer!"[1] Like many of the popes, he wrote on the subject for the edification of the faithful. In his 2002 Apostolic Letter *Rosarium Virginis Mariae* (The Rosary of the Virgin Mary) he urged, "Confidently take up the Rosary once again. Rediscover the Rosary in the light of Scripture, in harmony with the liturgy, and in the context of your daily lives" (*RVM*, 43). What a challenge! And from the Pope himself.

The Rosary gives so much more than what it takes in time and effort. In a very real sense, it serves as a catalyst to stir within us God's grace and peace, or an antenna, so to speak, with which it is easy to pick up the transmission of that grace directly to us, the intended receivers. After all, we have been equipped by our Creator with the ability to receive his Word and every expression of his love for us; ever since humankind was conceived in the mind of God, we have had the physical and spiritual capacity to "hear" him.

Pope John Paul II, his predecessors, and his successor, Pope Benedict XVI, have all recognized the power of receiving God's grace in our lives and how easy it really is to ask for that holy and healing touch, however unworthy any of us may be in the moment of asking. All the Lord wants from us is that we ask, that we make some kind of affirmative gesture or movement in his direction in response to his never-ending invitation, that we reach out like the ailing woman in the crowd to touch his garment (Mk 5:27). And the Lord is available to us, always and everywhere, along with his mother who stands with him and intercedes with him on our behalf. So little is required of any of us; we need simply turn to him.

This book, then, is an invitation to Christian men, and women as well. It's not only for Catholics, for the Rosary is not exclusively a Catholic prayer. I invite you to share the peace and joy that I and so many others for hundreds of years have experienced on this powerful journey. Join the worldwide community of prayer that is available to you in your own living room, backyard, or favorite church pew. The Rosary is an invitation from God—Father, Son, and Holy Spirit—and from the Mother of God, Mary, our Blessed Mother.

Walk with me—with us—on the path of prayer to peace. This is a path that leads directly to God himself, into the heart of the Trinity that is the source of all love and all peace. Isn't that what we are all seeking? Pray with other men of great faith and steadfast purpose; pray along with the women in your lives. We can learn from one another how to pray and why we pray, using the simplest and most beautiful tool the Lord has literally placed in our hands.

Some may hesitate, but can you give me any reason *not* to pray the Rosary? Why say "no" to one of the most precious gifts you will ever receive? Why not give it a try? As John Paul II wrote, it is "marvelous in its simplicity and in its depth" (*RVM*, 2). The suggestions contained in this little book can work as an aid in getting started. I ask only that you spend a little time reading about what has happened to me over the past several years, which I share in these pages as the reality of one man's experience. Also, I offer insights into what became for me a new world—or rather, a new perspective on the world—which I gained from standing still long enough to listen to Jesus, Mary, my pastor, my late mother, my wife, my bishop, and other men who have been placed in my life as God's messengers. They—like you—are the ambassadors of Christ in every minute and every aspect of daily life. My great learning has been saying "yes" to *you* and listening to *you*—and answering the Lord's call to serve *you* on our journey together to him.

In this book, you will learn about the mission of Real Men Pray the Rosary (RMPTR), the nonprofit ministry my wife and I founded to share the spiritual blessings of praying the Most Holy Rosary of the Blessed Virgin Mary with all Christians, especially men. Specifically, the mission statement of RMPTR is derived directly from the Apostolic Letter of Blessed John Paul II quoted earlier.

At RMPTR, we aim to "promote the Rosary with conviction, in the light of scripture, in harmony with the liturgy and in the context of our daily lives." I have reflected and prayed about this extensively, and I am grateful that this ministry or apostolate has gained a tremendous amount of traction with its simple, direct, and powerful message. Our goal is to keep devotion to praying the Rosary alive and well in our time. In a world filled with fast-paced distractions and ubiquitous technology, we endeavor to encourage people to unplug from time to time, sharing in something that doesn't need electricity or an LCD screen. Just clear the mind for prayer and meditation on the life and teachings of Jesus Christ. Perhaps even daily, as our Blessed Mother recommended at Fatima and as countless saints have done throughout their own journeys to holiness.

The Rosary has a body and a soul. The body of the Rosary is composed of the prayers. Some of those prayers are prayed in groups of ten, called a "decade." The Rosary invites us to contemplate twenty important points in the life and teachings of Jesus and his mother, Mary. These points make up the Rosary's soul and are referred to as Rosary Mysteries. As we pray the Mysteries, we contemplate how the biblical messages apply to our daily lives—and therein lies the Rosary's transformative power.

The Mysteries of each decade together embody the overall mystery of the Rosary, which is not something forever hidden or unknowable. On the contrary, the mystery of the Rosary is an invitation to discover something that we have not known before, to experience something that may be brand new or foreign to us. The mystery of the Rosary is a door, perhaps yet unopened, through which we are most graciously invited to pass. It may also present itself to us in the form of a familiar gospel story revealed to us in a new and different perspective. All we need do is open the door through prayer: knock, and it shall be opened to us (cf. Mt 7:7).

A couple of years ago, I was interviewed by a newspaper reporter. During the course of the interview, he tried to get me to agree with the notion that because I was so familiar with the traditional Rosary prayers, somehow those prayers were more tedious and less meaningful to me. He suggested that continually repeating them lulled me into some sort of meditative trance, and thus I didn't appreciate or understand the prayers any longer. On the contrary, I quickly corrected him, their familiarity was comforting and made them even more treasured to me. I feel the same way when hearing a loved one's comforting voice as when reciting those familiar prayers. For example, I told him, a mother's voice is usually one that we've heard thousands of times. That loving, nurturing voice that many of us are blessed to know and treasure does not become mundane simply because we've heard it before. No matter how many times we've heard it, we do not take it for granted.

Later, as I read more about the Rosary throughout history, I learned that one of the most famous popes, Pope Leo XIII, had described the familiarity of those prayers in much the same way over a hundred years ago: "The Rosary also floods the soul of those who recite it devoutly with an ever new sweetness of piety, giving them the impression and emotion as if they were hearing the *very voice of their most merciful Mother* explaining these mysteries to them and conversing with them at length for their salvation" (*MDM*, 17).

That familiarity evolves into an intimate dialogue with our Blessed Mother. Thus, when one is in the midst of deep prayer in the Rosary, Mary becomes spiritually present to meet us and lead us by the hand through each of those important points of meditation known as the Mysteries. When we pray the Rosary, we are permitted to live those Mysteries through her eyes, through her perspective. That is the beauty of the Rosary: to understand and live those twenty salient points in the life and teachings of Jesus and Mary, with Mary's familiar voice narrating the way.

Ad Jesum per Mariam. To Jesus through Mary.

Why the Rosary?

Pope Pius XII and his successors have referred to the Rosary as a "compendium of the Gospels." Perhaps because of my profession as an attorney, I view the Rosary as an "executive summary." And as an executive summary, it is a *short, condensed,* and *time-efficient path* to reflection on our spiritual life. In business, we find many important things presented to us in summary form: headnotes on newly reported cases in law, indexes of leading economic indicators for those who make long-term financial decisions, and abstracts of reports for those who study demographics or statistics.

The Rosary Mysteries provide an efficient entry point into the life of Jesus and Mary. We are called, in praying the Rosary, to focus on the four groups of Rosary Mysteries: Joyful, Sorrowful, Glorious, and—a recent addition—Luminous. These four groups provide an introduction into twenty specific and salient points in the teaching of Jesus.

Praying the Rosary daily allows us to live and experience the heights and the depths of our entire faith in less than a week's time. Praying the Rosary daily permits us, within a span of seven days, to personally visit the Holy Family as it was carefully nurtured and formed, to live with the Jesus who actually dwelt among us, to re-create and agonize with the sacrifice and strength of the Passion, and finally to celebrate the glory of a divine promise satisfied.

Studying the Bible passages by themselves could accomplish a coverage of the same material. But praying at the "school of Mary," to the drumbeat and the rhythm of the Hail Mary and the Lord's Prayer, enables one to see our Lord and experience our Christian faith through Mary's eyes—or at least with her *prayers for us*—as we meditate faithfully upon those Mysteries.

The Rosary presents our prayer life with an opportunity for structure that fine-tunes and leverages our spiritual energies in a more complete and comprehensive manner. For example, you could get off the couch and drive to the gym and, with a sense of determination, sit at the leg extension machine and work your quadriceps. While that effort would be good, or at least healthier than lying on the couch, it would be even more productive to sit with a trainer and be led through an organized and time-tested workout designed to strengthen and tone all of the muscle groups.

Such is the Rosary. Individuals who pray the Rosary regularly can call on Mary's intercession as a spiritual trainer to not just lead them in one isolated workout but rather to engage them to contemplate the span of the Christian good news in an organized way. Over time, as we visit the twenty faith points, or "Mysteries," in the teachings of Christianity, those points become engrained within us or, as the popes say, "inculcate" the faith. The Mysteries become a part of our very existence. We can't help but experience the "joy of the Christmas season" every Monday and Saturday when we meditate upon the third Joyful Mystery, the Birth of Jesus. Just like the couch potato who over time works off the years of inactivity through systematic exercise, so also our prayer life grows and gains muscle tone. In our spiritual workout, we also come to look forward to that twenty-decade journey.

The Rosary presents a point of entry into a study of the Christian good news. Praying the Rosary daily over a period of time permits us to integrate gospel lessons into our everyday lives. Each time we reflect on a Mystery, we interpret it in the light of our current place in life. As our life and circumstances change, so too does our interpretation of the Rosary. Most of us need daily nourishment, especially in the faith. And praying the Rosary is a way to nourish that faith.

For example, in the Sorrowful Mysteries, sometimes our focus is on the Lord's sacrifice for us. His physical suffering speaks to our own experiences of pain and discomfort. Understanding that Jesus endured that suffering for *us* out of love can also make us wonder if we have enough love to endure such trials for those whom *we* love or are called to love. At other times, we see these Mysteries through Mary's eyes and marvel at her supreme trust in the divine plan, which enabled her to watch as her beloved son endured such suffering. Yet there is no biblical reference to our Blessed Mother's complaints. For those of us who are parents, it is difficult to even imagine the anguish Mary endured in silently witnessing her son's suffering and yet fully trusting in God's salvific plan.

My Story: Mom Knows Best

I call this my "Saul conversion story," in which I was struck not by lightning but by a Rosary!

My dear and saintly mom, Alicia Vera Calvillo, always urged me to have a special love for our "Blessed Mother" and tried to teach me to pray the Rosary. But I was convinced the Rosary was for "old ladies and funerals." It was not for men—not for real men.

Then in the summer of 2008, I found myself at the lowest point in my life. My marriage was in tatters. Many of my fundamental beliefs about myself, my wife, and my marriage had been shattered. I felt like a failure. The prospect of my children living in a broken family was almost more than I could handle. I felt a sense of desperation. I felt a sense of hopelessness.

I instinctively knew I needed a spiritual recharge. I knew that I needed God's help for what may lie ahead in my life. I heard about a retreat for men called the ACTS retreat. Although I had heard of the retreat from other friends and acquaintances, it had never been the right time or the right place. Now was finally the right time.

After many exchanged messages, I met one of the retreat organizers at the parking lot of St. Joseph the Worker Church on a Saturday afternoon. I was impressed that he would take time away from his family on a Saturday afternoon to meet me—a total stranger—with very little notice, just to hand me an application to attend that retreat. I'll never forget him. He has become one of my heroes: Alex Gamboa Jr. (I share his story a bit later on, including how he was the inspiration for the Rosary-in-fist logo for Real Men Pray the Rosary.)

When the time came for me to leave for the retreat, my small children and my wife drove with me to the church. I sat in our minivan in the church parking lot literally trembling, as I wondered whether I could summon the courage to get down from the van. I sat there quietly for what seemed like an eternity. But when I saw my then-eighteen-year-old son Dave and my brother Bobby waiting there for us, I decided that, if they had come to the retreat "send-off" to show their support, I needed to give it a try. If they had not been there, I'm not sure if I would have attended the retreat. Bobby now says that he came to make sure I did go!

Before I left for the retreat, I consulted with various priest friends about the retreat, and they, especially Monsignor Gustavo Barrera, told me to "Let go and let God." Essentially, they were telling me to trust in God to help me through this challenging time in my life. I have always been a firm believer in the notion that you get out of something what you put into it. My dad has always preached that lesson. If you really want to learn how to do something and do it well, then you really need to try your absolute best. The same went for the retreat. If I was looking for some help from the Almighty, then I needed to let him help me through this retreat, if that was his will.

My wife, Valerie, unbuckled the kids from their car seats as I grabbed my bags. I had purchased a leather journal at our local Barnes & Noble bookstore. If I was going to attend this retreat, I wanted to harvest everything that I could from it. I wanted to crystallize my thoughts and find out exactly what God wanted me to learn. I wanted to distill from the experience a rescue plan for that point in my life. I hoped scribbling in the journal was going to help me do that.

That particular ACTS retreat was held at a Benedictine monastery in the middle of nowhere, in an isolated section along the Texas-Mexico border. You could literally hear coyotes howling at night within a couple of miles from the monastery. We were told by retreat leaders to watch out for the scorpions and the rattlesnakes. Others half-jokingly told us to watch out for human "coyotes" who might be passing through this remote stretch of rough border hill country.

The first morning of the retreat we woke up before the sun rose and were led in the dark by candlelight to a quaint and intimate prayer garden. Each of the retreatants was then handed a Rosary. Each retreatant was invited to lead one Hail Mary. The team members were to read the Mysteries and to lead the Our Fathers, and so on, until we had completed the Rosary. As we began to pray as one group, I slowly realized the wonder and beauty of what these men were doing before sunrise out here in the middle of nowhere. I began to weep. From deep within my chest, deep within my heart and soul, deep within my hurt, I marveled and wept at the indescribable, visceral joy of the sight of eighty men wanting to connect with God, earnestly asking for help to do good with their lives. I wept at the reality of eighty rough-looking men from all walks of life, humbly and sincerely raising their hearts and minds to God.

As I cried, I thought of my mom. I found myself lost in an ecstatic fog of prayer in which my thoughts, my very soul, were transported across time and space. I felt profoundly guilty for never previously having prayed the Rosary with my mom. I felt ashamed that I labeled this beautiful prayer the domain of "old ladies and funerals." I felt a prayerful happiness, a warm comforting presence.

As weird as it sounds, in this fog, I felt as though I was praying with everyone who had ever prayed the Rosary. I felt my grandmother Vera praying with me. I felt my mom. I felt the hearts of those eighty men. I felt like I was praying with and to Jesus himself as I stood at the foot of the statue of the Blessed Virgin Mary, her arms gracefully outstretched, in the center of this tranquil prayer garden.

All the while, I sobbed quietly, tears streaming happily and easily from my amazed eyes. My happy weeping caused my chest to heave with a gasp of God's reality.

Throughout the next two days of the retreat, the same miraculous scene unfolded each morning during the Rosary. Each time that we prayed the Rosary, eighty men huddled in the cozy prayer garden of that Benedictine monastery nestled in the middle of the South Texas brush country. Eighty men forgot their worries and their sinfulness and instead, during Rosary time, focused on asking our Blessed Mother to join with us, pray with us, and pray *for* us. Each time that we gathered to start our day, tears of pent-up emotions streamed down my cheeks as I prayed transcendentally with all Christians, all Catholics—through, with, and in Mary—to Jesus.

I prayed out of guilt for my sinfulness, my thoughtlessness, my recklessness, my apathy. I prayed out of love—a growing love. I prayed with rejuvenated faith. I felt the old David Calvillo being slowly but steadily revived and strengthened. I lived my "Saul conversion moment" every morning when we prayed the Rosary during that retreat. Put simply, I was being reborn (cf. Jn 3:3–5). ACTS saved my life. ACTS changed my life. The Rosary became my "sweet chain" linking me from the South Texas brush country —from my little corner of the world—to God himself.

As I wrote in that new leather journal, I sorted through the thoughts I was experiencing and tried to discern what lessons I was destined to glean from the retreat. My passionate scribblings slowly guided me to one unmistakable conclusion: Jesus Christ had to be at the center of my life, as nothing less than the first priority. The rest would take care of itself.

As the retreat came to its inevitable conclusion, I approached Nancy Boushey, a Benedictine residing at the monastery whom I knew, and confided in her that I wanted to purchase something from their small bookstore to give to the retreat team members as a token of my appreciation for the work and the love that they had invested. She smiled and lovingly led me to the gift shop tucked away in the corner of the main building, where I tried to determine whether there was a product of which there were enough in stock so that each retreat team member could receive a gift. As it turned out, there was only one item in the entire store of which they had enough. It was a book—a small, nondescript, innocuous-looking book. Although together all the books cost more than I had brought with me to the retreat, Sr. Nancy kindly let me have the books for whatever I could offer.

I went back to the residential dormitory area where my fellow retreatants were lounging and asked the others to join me in signing the inside covers of all of the books. That way, every team member would receive a book with the signatures of the retreatants. Each team member would know that they had touched the lives of these specific men. All the retreatants responded enthusiastically, and a mass book signing began.

I asked for time to address the retreat team on behalf of the men in attendance, offering our thanks during the closing ceremonies. Each retreatant selected a team member to personally embrace and hand him one of these signed books. This was the profound moment that ended the retreat.

There appeared to be one extra copy of that book. I thought I had counted properly, but for some reason, I had an extra. Oh well. I figured that I'd paid for them, so I could indulge myself and keep that extra as a memento. I stuck it in my luggage and forgot about it.

Afterward, I relished in the joy that I had felt during the ACTS retreat. I was excited to implement the lesson of the retreat by beginning a new life with Jesus Christ at its center.

Later, when I went through my bag of mementos from the retreat, I discovered that extra book from the monastery bookstore. I looked at the book, whose title had been largely unimportant to the purpose at hand, which was to acknowledge and express my gratitude to the men on the retreat team. It turned out the title and its author was another part of God's plan to rescue me: *The Secret of the Rosary* by St. Louis de Montfort! Despite being a cradle Catholic from a good church-going family, I had never heard of St. Louis de Montfort. But the Rosary, on the other hand, I had just discovered anew.

The Rosary was the path vividly opened for me during the retreat, and my mom's lessons that I had previously ignored were now front and center. Reading the book seemed like the natural next step for me in my new life's journey. Why else would that book, with that title, have been the only overstocked item in the bookstore? I picked up the book and began to read, growing in the excitement that this was clearly a part of the Holy Spirit's plan for me.

The Secret of the Rosary was slow reading. Every page, every paragraph, sometimes every sentence seemed to be filled with kernels of divine wisdom to be carefully and fully harvested. I read and reread sentences, digesting each thought.

Each "rose," as the chapters and sections are called, proved to be more enlightening than the next. I'd report back to my wife, "Wow. This book is amazing. It is a hard read but a beautiful one." I was stunned at how much I had not known about the meaning of the Rosary, of its biblical source, of its power.

St. Louis de Montfort holds nothing back. In his writings, he expresses the beauty of the Rosary in the same manner that a lover gushes with affection for a new love.

As I read through this book, I also began to read other materials about this French saint from the 1700s and found a small pamphlet at a local bookstore about the Total Consecration and St. Louis de Montfort's writings on Mary.

Shortly thereafter, I began joining my Knights of Columbus Council at their Rosary novenas. (I am currently a 4th Degree Sir Knight.) Although it was slightly different from the ACTS retreat, the core experience was the same: praying the Rosary with men. During one of those novenas, I noticed on one of the church's announcement bulletin boards a flyer about the start of classes on Total Consecration to Jesus through Mary according to the writings of St. Louis de Montfort. I tore the flyer off the bulletin board and took it home. I placed it prominently on the refrigerator and waited for the bait to take.

That evening my wife, Valerie, asked me, "What is this about?" I excitedly shared with her what little I knew. This was the same saint who wrote that amazing book on the Rosary, and this consecration thing was something to help us get closer to our Blessed Mother. I told her, "I'd like us to do it as a couple." Valerie, of course, said "yes."

Together we undertook the Act of Total Consecration to Jesus through Mary on August 15, the Feast of the Assumption, and we were sacramentally married a few days later on August 19. Thus, our marriage was consecrated through Mary from its sacramental beginning. It has been the joyous glue that has bound us together and since then has rewarded us with two beautiful baby girls. Our other five beautiful children, who have been swept along on this journey with us, have been amazed at the changes.

The next spring, I decided that I wanted to bring a Montfort priest to our diocese to help us share the joy of de Montfort's Total Consecration spirituality with others. I invited Fr. Hugh Gillespie, a priest belonging to the order founded by St. Louis de Montfort, to "God's country," our little corner of the world.

Around this time, my mother, who had been chronically ill for most of the previous twenty years, fell into her final illness. In early March, Mom left home for the last time to go into our local hospital. After a few weeks, we were counseled by her physicians to "let her go." My dad, after consultation with his beloved home pastor, emphatically responded: "We are Catholic. We are pro-life. Do everything you can for her."

During that Holy Week, the work we had begun with Real Men Pray the Rosary, Inc., was featured in *The Wall Street Journal*. I was able to share this bit of good news with my mom in the throes of her illness, and she was able to acknowledge the good work.

Mom endured close call after close call and then had a massive heart attack during dialysis. Once again the doctors suggested that we "let her go." That night I decided I was not going to leave her room. One of my aunts asked if she could join me. And my pastor, Fr. Alfonso Guevara, arrived in the late evening. He, my aunt, and I prayed the Rosary together as well as the Litany of the Saints. Fr. Alfonso explained that the Rosary and the Litany would ensure that Mary and the community of saints would be present to welcome my mom if it was indeed her time.

Mom hung on as long she could until finally she passed as we—her husband, her five children and daughters-in-law, and her three sisters—prayed the Rosary huddled around her bed. Within moments of her passing and our last "Hail Holy Queen," a faithful Filipino nurse suggested that if we were believers, it was a good time to pray the Divine Mercy Chaplet. Again, as a family, we prayed the Divine Mercy Chaplet as my saintly mother's soul passed from her earthly body.

Within moments of finishing the Divine Mercy Chaplet, I realized something. My mom was sending me one more lesson. My mom, who never gave up trying to guide her oldest son to pray the Rosary faithfully and to rely on our Blessed Mother for help, had one more message for her hardheaded son. Mom made sure that I knew how she and our Blessed Mother felt about our efforts, for she passed away on April 28, 2010—the feast day of St. Louis de Montfort!

Much more than "happy accidents," seeming coincidences reveal a divine hand at work in all our lives, in many ways, visible and invisible. With God's grace and open prayer, these experiences help us identify and appreciate his providential hand at work.

How to Pray the Rosary Now: A Practical Guide

> Rejoice always. Pray without ceasing. Give thanks
> in all things for this is God's will for you through
> Christ Jesus. (1 Thes 5:16–18)

St. Paul tells us to pray "without ceasing"! While that sounds like a nice ideal, it isn't realistic, is it? How can I pray all the time? I pray when I need to or when I'm really, really thankful for something, but *all the time?*

It *is* possible to "pray without ceasing." How? The Most Holy Rosary of the Blessed Virgin Mary.

In an Apostolic Letter, Pope John Paul II wrote that "The Rosary, in its own particular way, is part of this varied panorama of 'ceaseless' prayer" (*RVM*, 13). He confirms that we can achieve prayer without ceasing, with the aid of the Rosary. A variety of different ways exist to pray the Rosary; employing those ways can guide us toward the goal of weaving ceaseless prayer into our daily lives and our spiritual journey.

Grab it. Pray it. Just do it.

The easy—and the most typical—way that we can pray the Rosary is, as the Nike ad says, "Just do it." Grab the Rosary, and pray it. Some of us have a favorite Rosary, perhaps one that a family member gave us, and it is so pretty that we display it as a badge of our Catholicism or sometimes even as a decoration. But it is a prayer tool, first and foremost. Take that pretty Rosary, dust it off, and begin to pray with it. If you aren't familiar with the Rosary prayers and the Mysteries, then a Rosary pamphlet or a booklet is important to help guide your prayer. We will review the basics of how to pray the Rosary a little later in this book.

Most people begin by praying the Rosary alone at first. Praying by ourselves has the advantage of permitting us to dive deeply into our personal intentions. Without the distractions of coordinating prayers, verbal responses, or social interactions with others, we can focus solely on the prayers, the Mysteries, and those worries and dreams that impact our spiritual journey.

The prayer becomes almost visceral, possessing a kind of "physicality," as Pope John Paul II refers to it. The physicality comes from feeling through our fingers the touch of the bead that we use as a counting mechanism, as a textual road map to keep us on track in moving with our hands from one prayer to another and from one group of prayers to a faith point, or Mystery, and so on. The physicality also comes from touching that crucifix in our hand. Many popes have written that they prefer a crucifix on the body of the Rosary itself as opposed to an empty cross. One reason for that preference may be because running our eyes and fingers across the crucifix allows us to experience the corpus of the crucified Christ in a very personal veneration of our Savior. That experience of venerating our Lord has the potential to impact us in a way that few other methods of praying can. Merely touching and experiencing the body of Christ through the crucifix at the beginning and end of the Rosary provides a prayer in and of itself.

In additional to this physicality, there is the "rhythm" of the Rosary in our daily lives. This rhythm can manifest itself in the steady progression through the Rosary as the beads noisily rub against the pew or the bottom of the chair where we pray. The drumbeat of the Hail Mary prayers that we say within the Rosary provide the rhythmic foundation within which to experience the harmony and the song of the faith as set forth in chronological sequence through the Rosary Mysteries. The rhythmic familiarity of our Blessed Mother's call can console as we invoke her prayers with and for us.

The place where we pray can also be important. Choosing a prayer space within our house, our prayer garden in the backyard, in front of the Blessed Sacrament at our church, or at our office or school can help offer some variety once we have become accustomed to praying the Rosary. On the other hand, there is something comforting about adopting a routine and sticking to the same place or same time. Praying the Rosary can become an intimate, private oasis within our daily lives when we step into a prayer corner in our home and, within that space, retreat as Jesus advised: "When you pray, go into your room and shut the door and pray to your Father who is in secret" (Mt 6:6).

Grab your favorite Rosary, and just pray it . . . with a friend.

There is also something beautiful, however, about sharing a prayer with a friend. Sometimes, that beauty is magnified when we pray as a community. When most of us think of praying the Rosary, we probably think of funerals, when communities pray the Rosary in honor of the deceased. But as we'll see in this book, there are many other contexts for praying the Rosary, such as my own experience of the Rosary during an ACTS retreat.

The value of community adds a certain beauty to praying that is very catholic. It is catholic because it is indeed universal to want to come together, from all walks of life, to express ourselves in prayer. Praying the Rosary as a community is an extension of that Christian call to unite as the Body of Christ.

Many groups of men and women gather together regularly to pray the Rosary. The Knights of Columbus is such a group. In my own family, my dad is a fifty-year Knight, who has gone from a Grand Knight for his Council to now being a Faithful Navigator for his Assembly. My three brothers and I are 4th Degree Sir Knights and members of his Assembly. Many councils of Knights gather for novenas that follow the liturgical calendar. For example, prior to the Feast of Christ the King, the men will gather for those nine days leading up to the feast day to pray the Rosary specifically as a community of men. This fosters unity and leadership within the brother Knights and gives them a real sense of what it means to be part of the mystical Body of Christ. Such a sense is particularly powerful when we remember the words of Jesus himself: "When two or more are gathered in my name, there am I in the midst of them" (Mt 18:20).

Grab your Rosary . . . and pray it with music.

Another way to pray the Rosary involves audio or video recordings of the Rosary. These days many groups and even celebrities or well-known people have recorded themselves praying the Rosary. These recordings are available in Catholic book and gift shops in parish stores, and on Internet sites where music is purchased. Some are even available as podcasts or as DVDs.[2]

This method of praying the Rosary expands the opportunities that we have to pray the Rosary within the context of our daily lives, as John Paul II called us to do. Many people complain that they cannot carve out the time or find a special place in their homes, or elsewhere, to do so. In today's society, however, our vehicles can constitute an almost monastic cell. So many of us spend a significant portion of our lives commuting to and from work or running errands and the like. Such a regular and captive setting provides us with the opportunity to be within ourselves. We can listen to music, we can read a book, or we can pray. With recordings of the Rosary and an iPod or mp3 player, you can listen and pray while driving or commuting on the train. It is a great way to spend more time with God. If we're going to be in the world, we might as well do so while hanging out with Jesus and Mary—raising our hearts and minds in prayer.

Many people who take this kind of opportunity report that they actually look *forward* to their daily commute to and from work because it is the only time for prayer that their daily obligations permit, and they experience great joy within that time of prayer. Imagine that—looking forward to your commute!

Much joy derives from the varied Rosary recordings available. Some talented musicians and their affiliated musical groups, such as Vinny Flynn, produce beautiful music accompaniment to the prayer and elevate the prayer to such a level that St. Augustine might be inspired to comment, "He who sings well prays twice."

These recordings showcase the full range of Catholic musical talent, expressed in daily prayer. Others feature groups at events like men's conferences, who record their communal praying of the Rosary.

Listening or watching such recordings over a period of time can make them become so familiar that you begin to feel as if you are praying "with" the people in the recording. Or perhaps you really were at the conference recorded, and it allows you to relive your experience on retreat. In either case, this type of recording provides the opportunity for the Rosary to transcend time and geography by connecting the praying faithful who were recorded with the faithful listening to that Rosary later on. Once again, the Rosary is a "sweet chain" linking us not only to God himself but also to one another.

Recordings also provide a sense of flexibility. In today's world, it can indeed be difficult to commit to a block of thirty minutes for daily prayer. A Rosary recording very easily permits us to start and stop our praying of the Rosary when circumstances dictate. Sometimes we can begin the day with the first couple decades and Mysteries on the commute, squeeze in another decade during lunch or break, and then conclude the remaining decades on the return ride home. This method also has the advantage of permitting us to pause and digest the prayers that we've prayed up to a certain point and then to resume the spiritual nourishment later.

Grab it. Pray it . . . a little bit at a time.

Like the previous method, this way of praying the Rosary allows the person to weave their prayer into the fabric of an entire day—a decade here and a decade there—until the entire Rosary has been prayed. While some frown on that practice, others find it a great way to directly live the call to be in ceaseless prayer. By dividing the day into distinct parts, during which we find ourselves meditating upon certain Mysteries, this pattern permits us to weave prayer and the salient points of our Christian faith, which constitute the Rosary Mysteries, into our entire day or at least until the five decades and Mysteries are completed. In this way, we live a whole day filled with prayer; we hang out with Jesus and Mary the entire day.

Praying the Rosary over the course of the day in this way also permits us to invite others to share in part of our Rosary. It is hard enough sometimes to get ourselves to commit to praying the "full" Rosary—never mind asking others to pray with us. But sometimes those people might join us for a Mystery or two. In doing so, at least we've invited those folks into our prayer life for a day, and they will be impacted by that sharing.

Lingering with the Rosary over the course of the day is a good way to get closer to St. Paul's ideal of "praying without ceasing." You can do it.

Grab it. Pray it . . . on the run.

Some of us like to exercise. I've always loved to run. Some of my best thoughts occur while I run. Running is my way of exploring my neighborhood or a new city or a park. Running permits me to get to know a place from the ground up—one stride at a time.

I also always liked to play with numbers in my head when I ran. I would count my steps or count my breathing. With my handy running watch, I would calculate my split times or my pace or try to predict my finish time, etc. I was always playing with numbers while I ran.

Until I discovered the beauty of the Rosary. Once I discovered the joy of praying the Rosary, especially while running, I've never gone back to wasting my time by twirling figures around in my head. Instead, I pray the Rosary while I run. It adds a whole new level of accomplishment to be able to take that first step out of my house and begin my stride with the words "I believe in God the Father Almighty, Creator of heaven and earth. . . ." Once I recite those amazing words in my heart as I begin my run, I know that I'm going to run for at least thirty minutes; that I will be accompanied by our Blessed Mother, my spiritual trainer; and that my run that day will be a prayerful journey.

On Monday, it will be a journey where I run into the house and Mary tells me the story of this angel who came to tell her she would give birth to this amazing child-Savior, and then together we run "in haste" to visit her cousin, Elizabeth, and so on. All along my running trail, I am fully alive in the presence of God, present in prayer, raising my heart and mind to be in communion with our Lord. I have that extra spring in my step from knowing that I am doing something completely and totally wholesome and joyful. I am breathing. I am jogging. I am praying. I am reliving the gospel Mysteries in my mind. Short of preparing to receive and then actually consuming the Eucharist, I cannot possibly be more alive than when I am praying the Rosary while running. Obviously, the same can be said for praying it while walking.

It is not essential to carry a physical Rosary as I'm running while praying. Thankfully, I have ten fingers with which to count the proper number of Hail Marys, but if I linger and end up praying eleven, I don't think our loving Mother will be too disappointed. The presence of mind required to remember the sequence and content of the prayers without the aid of a physical Rosary helps trigger a different, more intense level of concentration on the content of the Mysteries themselves. Overall, praying while jogging or running is a more corporal way to pray the Rosary. Many times, it is my favorite way to pray it.

Or maybe it is just my current favorite way to pray the Rosary. The truth is that each of these ways has advantages. The important thing about these various methods is that they permit us to incorporate, in a structured way, the praying of the Rosary into the fabric of our daily lives. Utilizing and varying the ways in which we pray the Rosary keeps prayer fresh and vivid for us as we reach toward that ideal of ceaseless prayer.

THE TOOL BOX: SIMPLE EXERCISES TO JUMP-START PRAYING THE ROSARY

1. Do you own a bible? Get one for yourself. An example might be one that indicates it is a "New American Bible" or a "Revised Standard Version Catholic edition."

2. Maybe, like me, you are surprised to learn that the Rosary prayers and the Mysteries are derived directly from scripture. Open your bible to the Gospel of Luke, chapter 1, verses 26–45. Does that sound familiar? That is the first line of the Rosary prayer known as the Hail Mary or, as it is called in Latin, the *Ave Maria*.

3. Take a few moments to consider your prayer life. Do you pray every day? What time of day do you pray?

4. Men often say, "I pray to give thanks. Isn't that enough?" At other times, I hear: "I start my day at the crack of dawn, and once I get going, I don't get to stop until I hit the bed at night." What is holding you back to pray more?

5. I have found that making time to pray makes me stronger and more peaceful in a way that I'd not considered before. Identify three ways that you can carve out some time during your day to pray and talk to God about the good and the not-so-good things in your life.

CHAPTER 2

A PRAYER FOR MEN

Iron sharpens iron, so one man sharpens another.
—Proverbs 27:17

Of all forms of prayer, that of the Rosary is more than ever necessary, for it not only addresses itself to [Mary, our Blessed Mother] through whom it pleased God to send every grace to us, but more than any other prayer it bears the universal stamp of collective and familial prayer.
—Pope Benedict XV, *DAP*

Your Story

What is your experience with the Rosary? If you were raised Catholic, surely you were exposed to this prayer. It is possible—even likely—that you were not "turned on" by the Rosary, thinking it largely a female obsession, a "sissy" thing.

As I began writing this book, I asked a number of men about their personal experience with the Rosary. Below is one response that could be called "typical," a relatively common experience among Catholic men who are still faithful to the Church. This is what Patrick from New Jersey had to share.

> Having grown up a Roman Catholic, attending Catholic school, the Holy Rosary was always present in my life. In grammar school, May was a very important month, as it was the month of Mary. During this month, we said the Rosary at home, and as students, we took part in the May crowning. This was especially exciting because the

May crowning and subsequent Rosary took place during school hours, helping to shorten our academic hours.

Upon graduating grammar school, the Rosary became even more a part of my life. My mother enrolled me in a high school across the state, but our home hadn't yet sold. In order for me to start school, I had to live with another family in the area; my sister would stay with a different family. Every Friday, my mother and sister and I would drive back home together. And on Sunday nights, we did the same drive in reverse.

During this time, we would say the Rosary. It wasn't always easy for me to concentrate on the Mysteries we were on while saying the prayers. I remember riding in the passenger seat trying to focus, but my thoughts would soon intrude: *Okay, Jesus is being scourged at the pillar. He's being whipped, and blood is everywhere. His hands are tied. That's what my teacher told me when I complained about my grade, that "his hands are tied." I don't understand . . . oh, the pillar and sweat and blood.* Other times when we were driving late Friday or late Sunday, I'd start to nod off, usually catching myself but occasionally getting a nudge from my mother. I felt guilty when these things happened and would often try to say another Rosary later.

My devotion to the Virgin Mary and to the Rosary grew beyond that of those around me when I was stacking chairs following a church function. A priest I had never met approached me.

"How old are you?"

"Sixteen, Father."

"Would you be interested in going to Fatima in Portugal?"

"I'd love to, but there's no way I can afford it."

I had, of course, heard of Fatima before, the place where the Virgin Mary visited three young shepherd children. I had also seen statues of Our Lady of Fatima. It turned out that money wasn't an obstacle. And so, it was in Fatima that my devotion to the Rosary grew.

In 1917, Lucia de Jesus and her cousins Jacinta and Francisco Marto prayed the Rosary around mid-day, which was their usual custom. Immediately following the Rosary, the Virgin Mary appeared to them in the Cova di Iria beginning on May 13, 1917. The apparitions continued on the thirteenth of the month for six months, ending in October of that same year. During these apparitions, Mary implored the world to pray the Rosary every day and to pray for the conversion of Russia. She also asked the children to add a prayer to the Rosary, the English version being:

> Oh my Jesus, forgive us our sins, save us from the fires of hell; lead all souls to heaven, especially those most in need of thy mercy.

As I sat in daily conferences given by Fr. Fox, who had led tours to Fatima for some time, my devotion to and love of the Mother of God grew. Every day of the trip, we said the Rosary and learned more about the apparitions of Fatima. We learned that there were three secrets, two of which had been revealed. The first secret was a vision of hell, and the second was a prediction of the end of World War I and the start of World War II. It wasn't until 2000 that the third secret was revealed: the prediction of the assassination attempt on the life of Pope John Paul II. I also had the opportunity to walk on my knees about a thousand feet on the marble path to the shrine while saying the Rosary.

This is the way many pilgrims finish their journeys, some of which last hundreds of miles, with a thousand feet on their knees as they pray the Rosary. While many used padding for their knees, I did not in order to make my suffering greater. (After doing this once, I realized that walking on knee pads was suffering enough.) I offered up my suffering for the sinners for whom I was saying the Rosary.

Another message that Mary gave to the children was to pray for the conversion of Communist Russia. This would require the fall of the Soviet Union. In 1986, the world was still mired in the Cold War, and the United States and the USSR were embroiled in a bitter arms race.

I scoffed at the idea that there would ever be religious freedom in Russia but prayed anyway. To my amazement, in 1989, the Soviet Union did indeed fall.

Following my return from Fatima, my devotion to Mary and the Rosary continued. I said the Rosary every night when I got into bed, often times going through all five Mysteries. I would sometimes fall asleep as I used to do in my car. I would pray to see an apparition of the Virgin Mary outside of my window. As my devotion continued to deepen, my Rosary beads became as important to me as gold. While making long trips with my mother and sister, we would pray the Rosary with the added prayer I brought them from Fatima.

In adulthood, however, I did not continue to pray the Rosary. My life changed, my beliefs evolved, and my religious practice grew less important to me through college and later years. I think that is probably true of many people. But now, being married and the father of a beautiful baby girl, I am in a very different place spiritually. Also, my relationship with the Church is very different now than it was when I was a child—or than it was even five or ten years ago. For one thing, my father died when I was very young, leaving my mother and six kids behind. It was pretty wild by the time I was a teen. But as my siblings also matured and started families of their own and as my mom retired from her job as a teacher, we found our way spiritually—most of us either remaining in or returning to the Church as our spiritual home.

My wife converted to the Catholic faith, and we are hugely grateful for the role that faith and Church play in our lives—and the young life of our first child.

The stories of men like Patrick in this book—and your story— tie back to my own story and link us all in the circle of faith that is so powerfully represented by the Holy Rosary, the simplest and most profound of prayers.

A Spirituality for "Real Men"

Male spirituality, or "masculine" spirituality, is a term often used these days by Christians who want to understand and encourage real spiritual development in men of faith. The term can mean almost anything you want it to mean. I have thought a lot about it over the past several years, and I want to lay out my concept for you, without overcomplicating it.

For me, behind the mission of Real Men Pray the Rosary is the idea that male spirituality is very real and important but not separate from the spirituality of women; rather, it is complementary, and necessarily so. I think it is valuable to *emphasize* male or masculine spirituality for men who are seeking an added dimension to their faith lives, a solid grounding from which they can grow ever stronger in love of God and service to their families.

Christian teaching is already so dynamic and muscular that it's not difficult to find aspects of the faith that appeal to men as "real men." But the so-called feminine aspects, such as devotion to the Blessed Virgin Mary, can be seen as a harder "sell" when it comes to Catholic men. As I have noted before, we can tend to dismiss Mary and the Rosary—and other manifestations of feminine presence in prayer and worship—as not manly enough for our tastes.

With the authority of my own experience as a Catholic man and that of many other men I know, I can say that there is no reason to fear or avoid the influence of feminine spirituality—in fact, just the opposite. Women complement and highlight our masculinity in matters temporal and spiritual alike.

Being a man is merely a starting point for those of us who are born that way. Just like Adam and every male since, each of us was created by God to be a unique person and to love and serve our Father with every fiber of our being—as men in this world. God has ordained that men and women balance and support one another in their roles in family and society. We need one another. We naturally love one another. We form the ideal partnership as friends, lovers, parents, helpmates, partners, and mutual pillars of support in every way. Understanding our complementary roles in spiritual matters draws us even closer to the women in our lives. We can further understand and depend upon one another if we know these interlocking and strengthening roles.

Jesus himself showed us the way. He lived a life so unique and independent but at the same time so utterly dependent upon those around him—especially women, such as his beloved mother and female friends, relatives, and disciples. After all, who stood at the foot of the Cross in Jesus' last moments of agony before he died? The women.

We see ourselves as men of action, decisive, courageous, "in charge." Often, those characteristics will define our roles in the contemporary world. But if we act and teach and direct others with *faith* in our hearts, how much more effective we will be! How much more like Jesus we will be.

As men, we are taught to "handle things," "fix it," "think it through," and the like. We are taught to "make things happen." We are not usually taught to seek help. That is why the typical stereotype is of the man who will wander around aimlessly for hours rather than ask for a map or seek directions. The stereotype is a bit much, but nevertheless, the message is not far off. It does hit home for some of us: we are largely expected to rely on ourselves. As a result, when things happen to go well for us, some of us erroneously conclude that we have done so because we are "self-made men." That is, of course, a delusion to which men cling as they sort through the checklist of things needed in order to be "real men" on society's terms.

Only by consulting with and assiduously addressing the items on that checklist can we be successful "real men" in today's society. The truth is that we are not any more "self-made" than we were "self-made" in the womb. Rather, we are made by God him*self*. We are told that we are the only beings in God's creation that were created in "his own image" (Gn 1:27). We need to see through society's brainwashing and recognize that as "real men," if we truly want to "handle things," we are compelled to consult Jesus's checklist and to follow the only instruction manuals that truly count: the Bible and the teachings of the Church.

The Bible, especially the New Testament, offers a clear model for what "real men" should do. When Jesus realizes that his time is near, he doesn't devolve into checking his "to-do" list and ticking off how he is going to address his coming Passion and Crucifixion. Instead, what he does first is raise his heart and mind to the Father. He brings his closest friends with him to his favorite prayer garden, falls upon his knees, and calls upon his Father in prayer (Mt 26:36–42).

When we pray the Rosary on Tuesdays or on Fridays, this scene is the Sorrowful Mystery known as the Agony in the Garden (Mt 26:36–46). Jesus, the first "Real Man," gives us his divinely human example of an action that counts toward truly fixing things. He asks for guidance.

Jesus directly guides us to his three-point checklist: ask, seek, knock (Mt 7:7). Thus, real men—who need to find solutions to their chronic unemployment, guidance in parenting recalcitrant young adults, answers for comforting sick children, or ways to cope with the sad loneliness created by a spouse with a hidden life—are clearly directed by Jesus. He shows us not to withdraw within ourselves, not to "go it alone." Rather, he plainly tells us to ask his Father for the strength, for the answers, and for the door to be opened.

The best thing we can do for our families and for our children, then, is not to think that we can handle things by ourselves, to pull ourselves up "by the bootstraps" or "suck it up." Rather, the absolute best thing that we can do for them and ourselves is to pray.

Pray like Jesus did. "Now more than ever is the time to recall to mind what our Lord Jesus Christ wanted to teach us by his example: when he was in agony, he prayed the longer," wrote Pope Leo XIII in his Apostolic Letter *Salutaris Ille* (*SI*, 2). All else falls short if we don't start and end there—on our knees, in prayer to the Father, "with a crucifix in the right hand and the Rosary in the left and the holy names of Jesus and Mary in [our] heart."[1]

Alex Gamboa Jr.

Throughout the book I will share with you stories of men whose lives or example have touched me deeply and become a part of my own continuing journey as a man of faith. Among them is Alex, the always smiling, soft-spoken, shaved-headed leader of the "Cross Bearers," a motorcycle ministry that he cofounded with other local bikers.

This is the story of my encounter with him. It was a Saturday afternoon, and as we were talking, something inside me drove me to interrupt him. "Alex, I'd really like to make sure that a spot on your retreat is available for me, so I'd like to get that application and complete it in time for Mass tomorrow." Sensing my urgency, Alex responded without hesitation, "Sure. I'll meet you at the church parking lot on the south side of the church at three o'clock. Will that work for you, brother?"

I was a little surprised at his quick response and his willingness to take the time. I know how precious Saturday afternoons are for me. After working long days all week, Saturday afternoons are my special time with my children. Yet, Alex responded very directly and very positively. He was ready to serve and help me with the application. Maybe he knew I needed something, or maybe his own experience of the Rosary made him want to share that with me. Alex Gamboa Jr. stands today as one of my personal heroes largely because he gave up time on a precious Saturday afternoon to meet me—a stranger—and provide me with an application to attend an ACTS retreat, an experience that would save my life and, I pray, change it forever.

Alex's imprint on me extends beyond that monumental experience, though. Alex and a curious practice of his served as the inspiration for the logo that vividly transmits the message "Real Men Pray the Rosary" to the world. The Rosary-in-fist logo has Alex as its first model. After I attended that fateful ACTS retreat as a retreatant, I was asked to serve on a men's Spanish ACTS retreat team where Alex served as a team member. We were now working alongside each other to repeat the encounter with the Holy Spirit for another forty retreatants. Our retreat team meetings took place once a week for sixteen weeks. For four months, I observed Alex and the other men in a fraternal, prayerful setting; its impact exceeded even that of the retreat experience for me. It brought full circle the encounter with the Holy Spirit that had begun on my own retreat a few months earlier.

Alex had a very curious habit at those team meetings, a habit that I noticed extended beyond those meetings to the few occasions when I would see him in other settings. Alex always carries his Rosary wrapped around his hand. He wraps it around his wrist and his fist and secures the crucifix in the wrappings so that the Rosary becomes one with him. It truly becomes a part of him. When that Rosary melds itself into him like a tattoo, he physically becomes the embodiment of St. Paul's exhortation to "pray without ceasing." When asked about his habit, Alex would say that he just felt better that way. He felt better praying the Rosary while having it close to him at all times. It became almost second nature to him. Through this practice, Alex made it clear that he had a very special place in his heart and in his own spiritual journey for the Rosary.

One night, after having observed Alex with the Rosary on his fist for several months—and inspired by a couple of other men on the retreat team who prayed the Rosary devoutly and unashamedly—I looked around and suddenly a thought sparked within me: "real men pray the Rosary."

All of a sudden, my myopic and ignorant belief that the Rosary was for "old ladies and funerals" was ignited into a different reality. True men. Good men. Men of valor. Men of faith. Men of service. Men of love. Men praying the Rosary. Real men prayed the Rosary!

At the conclusion of that meeting, I couldn't drive home fast enough. An inspired spark ignited within my heart. I needed to form some sort of an organization based on this reality, with a website and a very specific logo. That organization would be called "Real Men Pray the Rosary," after the realization that struck me that night. The logo, the sign that would draw in people from all walks of life, would be that same sight that had caught my attention in one of my personal heroes: Alex Gamboa Jr. The Rosary in fist would be its symbol. Its mission would be to reach out to other knuckleheads like myself who were ignorant of the beauty and the power of the Rosary.

As a child of the 1970s, I grew up with symbols of power, sometimes militant power. The civil rights movement of the late 1960s and early 1970s in the United States spawned the "Chicano Power" movement in the southwest United States and the "Black Power" movement in other parts of the country; both movements symbolized the empowerment of previously disenfranchised people. Those movements were represented by the closed and raised fist. The closed and raised fist served as a sign that things were going to change. These people were now passionate and empowered, and they were not afraid to express it.

The Rosary-in-fist logo is an even more powerful symbol, a Christian expression that moves strongly beyond mere passionately militant energy. Prayer power. Rosary power. Men, who may have felt disarmed by a society that denigrates praying men, can now passionately and maybe even militantly rally around a symbol of strength, a symbol that profoundly communicates by its sheer simplicity: "I am empowered. I am not ashamed to display it." In this case, the empowerment springs from the true power that only prayer can instill, which is then magnified by the sight and example of a strong praying man. As Jesus himself showed, when the going got tough, the tough got to praying. Jesus, when faced with the imminent Passion and Crucifixion, got on his knees and prayed to his Father.

It is worth repeating the inspired words of Pope Leo XIII from 1883: "Now more than ever is the time to recall to mind what our Lord Jesus Christ wanted to teach us by his example: when he was in agony, he prayed the longer." Jesus' lesson is to become empowered through prayer and to persevere in prayer.

Alex Gamboa Jr. personifies a potent reality not only by sporting the Rosary around his fist as he does but, more importantly, by actually praying that Rosary. In doing so, his prayer practice shapes him into a role model for those of us fortunate enough to know him, pray with him, and serve our Lord with him.

Joe Connors's Secret

Another man whose influence has touched me in an enduring way is Joe Connors III, who wanted to continue the legacy of quiet evangelization begun by his father. In the process, Joe Connors III, became an instrument of God's plan and gently touched the lives of many people in an enduring way.

His father, Joe Connors Jr., was an FBI agent and a career law enforcement officer who lived in the DC area. He was also a devout Catholic and a dedicated believer in the power of the Rosary. Joe had a secret. He would buy copies of St. Louis de Montfort's *The Secret of the Rosary* and place them anonymously in the back of DC-area churches. He would leave them there, knowing that the power of the book's title would summon the faithful to pick up a copy. And a few of them would be compelled to read the book, allowing themselves to be impacted by the enlightened words of that sixteenth-century Marian saint.

Joe Jr.'s son never knew about his father's secret until after his father's death, when his beloved mother—a Secular Carmelite for forty-eight years—told him how Joe Jr. had led an unassuming, secretly evangelical life.

Inspired by that legacy, Joe Connors III, ironically a criminal defense lawyer, resolved to revive and perpetuate his father's quiet legacy. After attending and serving in a series of ACTS retreats, he began to buy *The Secret of the Rosary* directly from the publisher in quantities of five hundred at a time. Now, in deep South Texas on the Texas-Mexico border, Joe III, a fifty-something-year-old lanky, self-styled "workaholic," anonymously delivers copies of *The Secret of the Rosary* to churches in the area. His wife and children occasionally think he's crazy because he spends chunks of money buying books for people he'll never meet. But Joe III doesn't mind because he knows he is continuing the good work that his father began namely propagating faith in the power of the Rosary. At last count, Joe III had personally distributed about five thousand copies of St. Louis de Montfort's *The Secret of the Rosary*.

Included in the groups of area churches and chapels where he has quietly tendered these books is the Benedictine Monastery of the Good Shepherd, north of Rio Grande City, Texas. Joe III provides these books for use in the bookstore at the monastery as a way of helping the resident religious sisters raise funds for their continuing ministries. The monastery is a very popular place for spiritual retreats, especially ACTS retreats.

As I mentioned earlier, when I wished to tangibly express my gratitude to the men who had organized and executed my own ACTS retreat, I purchased copies of the book at that same monastery gift store. After discovering that I had bought an extra copy, I began to read it. That book that had been humbly donated by Joe Connors III added texture to the ecstatic experience of my ACTS retreat, and it opened up the substance of the Rosary in a profound way that continues to this day. It introduced me to

St. Louis de Montfort, all of whose works I have now read and devoutly attempt to practice.

I have often said that ACTS saved my life; ACTS changed my life. The Rosary provided and continues to provide that lifeline, that "sweet chain" to rescue me—oftentimes, from myself.

The Connors' father-son "Secret" served as an instrument in God's plan to save me from myself. My sentiment toward Joe can best be expressed in the words of St. Louis de Montfort: "May the perfect joy of Christ reign in your heart."

David Lerma's Prayer

David Lerma is known as "Animal." David is as wide as a brick wall and probably even more solidly built. With forearms as thick as telephone poles, a permanent sunglass tan line around his eyes, and a powerfully bald head; at first glance, he's an imposing figure. The truth is that although it is difficult for anyone to say "no" to him, it is probably because he is more prone to smile and bear-hug you than he is to physically threaten you.

This smiling bricklayer is known as "Animal" in the local construction industry because of his work ethic. David's work ethic is legendary because he works harder and longer than men half his age.

That same devotion and passion has found a new outlet. After a life-changing ACTS retreat in 2007, David started directing his boundless energy into service and prayer, specifically Rosary prayer and its healing power.

David is the leader of a group of men known informally as the "Prayer Warriors of South Texas." He and a group of varying number, from eight to upwards of fifteen, dedicate themselves to praying the Rosary for healing. The men come from diverse backgrounds: science teacher, construction superintendent, electrician, house painter, community activist, repo man, retired Marine sergeant. They share a common heritage—all brothers in Christ who lived an ACTS retreat—and resolved to devote their lives to prayer. Their efforts are part healing rosary and part educational ministry.

David and his band of rough, tough-looking Catholic men are "booked" by families throughout the region to join in the group's healing Rosaries. They are booked for months in advance for their standard Thursday evening sessions. They are also called in on an "emergency" basis when urgent prayer is warranted for an acutely ill person or someone in dire need of a "prayer intervention." They've prayed as a group in living rooms, kitchens, and backyards. They've also prayed in hospitals and retreat team meetings. Their ministry has continued now for several years.

Their Rosaries always inspire those they visit, and the men who pray have also been inspired as they've witnessed what many claim are healing miracles. They've prayed over and joined families in "laying hands" on cancer patients, heart attack victims, and those with clinical depression. Many families claim that after a prayer session with the Prayer Warriors, their previously sick family member has recovered or is well on the road to recovery. David and the guys are quick to point out, however, that if any healing or miracle occurred, it was accomplished through the power of the Holy Spirit and serves God's divine will.

They willingly assume the leadership role during their prayer sessions, yet they gently but firmly insist that everyone present participate in the Rosary. Although the Rosary is the "standard" Rosary—following the Mystery of the day: Joyful, Luminous, Sorrowful, or Glorious—they also weave in catechesis. The teaching aspect involves the power of prayer and the biblical source of the Rosary prayers and Mysteries. Mostly, though, they teach through their powerful example. The continuing presence of these dozen or so strong men, bound together by a firm belief in the power of raising hearts and minds to God, in the community of the living Body of Christ is the strongest and most enduring lesson.

In homes and communities throughout South Texas, David Lerma and the Prayer Warriors of South Texas vividly demonstrate the power of real men praying the Rosary.

JM and Mary, His Business Partner

JM is a pillar of the community. He earns a good living in the real estate business as a builder and a developer. Although naturally reserved and a serious gentleman (especially when he needs to be), the slightly built seventy-something-year-old is also known to share a quick smile. JM is somewhat shy, so you will not find him willingly at the center of attention or prone to making speeches, even among friends. When he does speak, however, people listen.

Service to the church is one of his central passions. He serves on several church-related committees, and these don't involve pushing paper or endlessly studying things. Instead, JM makes dream projects come to life—sometimes seemingly out of nothing. Countless projects have suddenly become a reality once JM becomes involved. On the committees where JM serves, he offers his expertise and his ability to make things happen.

JM is also a profoundly and sincerely humble man. He knows the source of his talents and success. To those who look beyond the obvious, they're as likely to see his fingerprints on a diocesan construction committee plan as they are to see his fingerprints on a broom sweeping a retreat hall at the end of a long day or setting up endless rows of stackable chairs before morning Mass during one of his beloved ACTS retreats. It is particularly fitting that JM's construction company built the main retreat house a year or so before he actually attended a retreat at that site in 2008. JM was a fellow retreatant on my ACTS retreat.

His most vivid testimony is the way he leads his life. Several years ago, JM consecrated his life to Jesus through Mary according to the Total Consecration writings of St. Louis de Montfort. This spirituality, which Pope John Paul II said "changed his life" and which served as the basis for his papal motto *Totus Tuus*, provides for a total consecration of oneself to Mary so that she can lead us to her son, our Savior.

For JM, this means that he does everything for Mary. JM and his wife like to go to adoration of the Blessed Sacrament together. He says that he likes to pray the Rosary during adoration and then pray more generally. With the challenging economic times, JM recently found his mind drifting during his post-Rosary prayers to matters of his construction business. He caught himself after a while and at first felt guilty. The more he thought about it, though, he came to the realization, "It's okay. Mary is my business partner." JM has consecrated his business to Jesus through Mary. In his heart, JM has established that everything he does—including his successful business—is through, with, in, and for Mary so that she may in turn give it to Jesus. It seemed only natural for JM to mull over the business issues he was facing in front of the Blessed Sacrament because he wanted and needed our Lord's guidance. Indeed, meeting the Lord in his Real Presence in dialogue during that session was more than "okay."

Mary is JM's business partner. JM is a role model for all of us. To Jesus through Mary.

One of the many lessons that I have learned in my recent spiritual journey is that not only is the Rosary for everyone, but there are also many who pray the Rosary who can serve as wonderful examples of prayerful leaders. The gentlemen featured on the preceding pages are just a small sample of such men—men who corrected my ignorance and enlightened me, men of prayer who are present in all of our lives. We just need to open our eyes and our hearts to see them and be inspired by them.

Mary, Jesus' Gift of Maternal Love

One of the themes that my own spiritual journey has taken me toward recently is an examination of the question: "Why our Blessed Mother?" As many commentators have observed, the Holy Spirit's presence seems stronger in women, and that may explain why they are more likely to develop a devotion to our Blessed Mother.

But why a Marian devotion for *men*?

One reason why we men should graciously invite our Blessed Mother into our heart stems directly from the fact that Jesus was a man—just like us. God chose to make Jesus a man. And God chose for him to be born of a woman. Thus, God developed in Jesus a relationship that is as strong as anything in heaven or on earth: the love of a son and his mother. Jesus had a distinct bond of love with his mother. Every fiber, every cell, every inch of him was connected in a primal way to his mom—just like many of us are blessed to be lovingly connected with our own earthly mothers.

That connection is strong and passionate. For example, if someone "messes with" or insults our mother, that evokes an emotion within us that is as visceral as any other emotion that we possess. The instinctive emotion evolves into anger and usually stirs us to action, which sometimes expressed in a not necessarily loving way. That same passion derives from a primal, profound love: maternal love. By acknowledging and appreciating the love that we share for our own heavenly mom, we confront the reality of Jesus' own relationship with Mary. Jesus was a man like us. He loved Mary not because the fourth commandment required all good Jews like himself to honor their mothers, but rather because she bore, nurtured, and raised him.

As an integral part of his final dramatic mission, Jesus Christ then, from the cross itself, climactically bequeathed to us his mother (cf. Jn 19:27). He gave us Mary to be our constant companion. He gave us his mother so that we could always feel that deep love, always. He gave us his mother so that we could better understand the love of a mother and a son. We could share, with Jesus Christ himself, in that profound love.

Humans are never permitted to look directly upon the face of God himself. The great Moses, the Lawgiver, is one exception. Although he initially encountered God through a burning bush, he was eventually permitted to gaze upon God "face to face" (cf. Ex 33:11). Even the great prophet Isaiah was only permitted a glimpse of God's garment (cf. Is 6:1). And that was enough to catalyze Isaiah's prophetic ministry. Thus, the best that most of us can generally hope for is, through grace, to occasionally be permitted a glimpse of God.

If "God is love" (1 Jn 4:16), then we can understand God better when we live in love. When we live out and understand love, when we love, we are permitted a glance at God, who *is* love. We can understand Jesus the man better also because that same tender, unshakable love we feel for our own mother is the same reality that Jesus lived and then bequeathed to us. We can love like Jesus of Nazareth loved. We can love like Jesus Christ loved.

That reality opens up all kinds of possibilities. It provides me with hope that even I, if I can love like Jesus loved in *this* way—love Mary like Jesus did—I can also live that universal Christ-like love that we are all called to live. You and I can love like Jesus Christ loves.

This is one of the greatest gifts of sharing his Blessed Mother. This gift is a joy so basic that even we knuckleheads can begin to understand and appreciate its significance.

These thoughts had been percolating inside me as I faced the loss of my own mother on April 28, 2010—providentially, as I wrote earlier, the feast day of St. Louis de Montfort, author of *The Secret of Mary* and *The Secret of the Rosary*. After her passing, these two books—which already had become seminal works for me—profoundly opened up the power of the Rosary to me and touched me with a new, tender way of finally appreciating Mary, the Mother of Jesus, the Mother of God. Although my mom, while she was alive, always counseled that we needed to honor and pray with Mary, it was a message I didn't understand. For my mother to have passed on the feast day of St. Louis de Montfort is a testament to God's clear message to me of the importance of Mary.

Amazing how God works. Jesus gave me his mother to, among other things, help me deal with the loss of my own beloved mom. So as not to feel alone. To always feel that irreplaceable, amazing maternal love. To understand how much God loves me. To bring me closer to Jesus Christ himself. To share more fully in his life. How can I not be eternally grateful and love and glorify my God for that perfect gift?

To Jesus through Mary . . . *Holy Mary, Mother of God, pray for us.* . . .

This is the key for us, for men who wish to experience a true conversion as taught by the Catholic Church and as lived by men and women, especially the saints, through the ages. One of my new favorite saints, St. Louis de Montfort, whom I discuss later, calls this special insight the "secret" of Mary. In fact, he wrote a book appropriately titled *The Secret of Mary*. With that book, St. Louis de Montfort has helped me order my thoughts on my love for our Blessed Mother.

In this book, I have invited you to come with me into the world of the Rosary, which is a special devotion to the Blessed Mother—already a perilous path for some "real men" who have always associated the Rosary with little old ladies in darkened church pews and found in it little relevance to a man's life. But true devotion, as practiced and understood fully in the Christian faith, means simply a strong commitment to that faith that is demonstrated in prayerfulness. It does not mean that you have to go around with your head hanging down and hands clasped together always. No, it means that you are always open to being touched by the Holy Spirit in a special way that will change and uplift you.

THE TOOL BOX: SIMPLE EXERCISES TO JUMP-START PRAYING THE ROSARY

Think for a minute: How would you choose a Rosary for yourself? As men, we don't want to handle things that are too easy to break or tear. We'd probably like a Rosary that could handle our day-to-day activities, one that we could stick in a pocket and not worry that we're going to reach in and pull out a broken string and have fifty-plus beads rolling around. Are you good with your hands? Could you make one? My dad will testify that I was probably the worst knot-tying Boy Scout in the history of the scouting movement, but somehow or other, I can now tie knots. If I can learn to make Rosaries with knots, so can you. I love the Rosaries that I learned to make at www.rosaryarmy.com because Rosaries that I make myself in that way, with nylon twine, will never break. I'm proud of how durable they are. I hope my prayer life will be as durable as the Rosaries I make.

1. Get out your tool box. Can *you* make a Rosary that is durable and feels good in your hands? If your Rosary is going to be your tool for praying, shouldn't it be a high-quality tool?

2. Think about the people you care about in your life. Who are you "responsible" for? Pray for one of these people.

3. As you think about your life, consider what *you* need. Do you need to be a better husband, a better father? Do you need patience to deal with that jerk who always seems to annoy you in the worst way? Do you need to hang out with people who share the values you admire? Pray for these needs that *you* have.

CHAPTER 3

A HISTORY OF THE ROSARY

> He who knows how to pray well, knows how to
> live well.
>
> —St. Augustine

> We have pointed out that the origin of this prayer
> is divine rather than human. We have shown how
> it is a wonderful garland, woven of the Angelic
> Salutation, interspersed with the Lord's Prayer,
> combined with the obligation of meditation. It
> is a most excellent manner of praying and very
> fruitful for the attainment of eternal life.
>
> —Pope Leo XIII, *DT*, 3

The Rosary is both timeless and timely. It is timely because it is timeless. It is timeless because it is always timely.

Over the course of Church history, when she has been under attack—by heresies, by military campaigns, by corrupt governments, or by internal struggles, indeed whenever the Church has needed it—praying the Rosary has proved timely and "efficacious" for the Church. The faithful throughout the ages have prayed the Rosary for the Church within time and just in the nick of time. Thus, it is timeless and timely.

A great source for history and insight, *The Catholic Encyclopedia* (the "old" edition published in 1913), describes the Rosary by referring to the Roman Breviary's description of it: "The Rosary . . . is a certain form of prayer wherein we say fifteen decades or ten of Hail Marys with an Our Father between each ten, while at each of these fifteen decades we recall successively in pious meditation one of the Mysteries of our redemption."[1]

While this is a very accurate description, the question is, "How did the Rosary become what it is today?"

The Origin of the Rosary

The Rosary has a long and often unclear history. In fact, the concept of "prayer beads" was instituted long before the advent of the Most Holy Rosary of the Blessed Virgin Mary.

So where did the Most Holy Rosary of the Blessed Virgin Mary come from?

Today, when we consider the origin of the Rosary, we typically think of either the St. Dominic story or the story of the 150-prayer Psalter.

According to Catholic tradition, the Virgin Mary appeared to St. Dominic in the year 1214 in the church of Prouille, France, and presented him with the Rosary. Indeed, many popes supported the belief that Dominic received the Rosary. As *The Catholic Encyclopedia* notes, "That many popes have so spoken is undoubtedly true, and amongst the rest we have a series of encyclicals, beginning in 1883, issued by Pope Leo XIII, which, while commending this devotion to the faithful in the most earnest terms, assumes the institution of the Rosary by St. Dominic to be a fact historically established."[2]

The traditional St. Dominic story is one that is mentioned most often in books on the Rosary or in papal documents. In this legendary story, our Blessed Mother gave the Rosary directly to St. Dominic as a weapon to use in combating heresies that were present in Europe at that time. As a result of the direct charge from our Blessed Mother, St. Dominic created the Dominican order, and then he and his order, the Friars Preachers, propagated the devotion to praying the Rosary throughout Europe. The overwhelming and successful response from the people in thirteenth-century Europe saved the Church from the heresy, and the reputation of the Rosary devotion grew.

Another story of the origin of the Rosary is the 150-prayer Psalter. This story traces the Rosary's origin to medieval farmers living near monasteries; they wished to emulate the monks who would beautifully and harmoniously chant the 150 Psalms. Doing so was not practical or even possible for some of the illiterate faithful who nevertheless wished to join in the beauty of such a fervent period of prayer. They thus began the practice of repeating 150 Our Fathers, and they kept count at first by counting 150 pebbles in a bag and then eventually 150 pebbles on a string.

Over time, the Angelic Salutation, or as we know it, the Hail Mary, grew more popular as the preferred prayer to recite as part of the "Rosarium," or collection of prayers. Eventually, clerics began to encourage meditation on the gospel, and thus the three traditional groups of Rosary Mysteries evolved: Joyful, Sorrowful, and Glorious. The 150 prayers were equally divided into three sets of fifty each. The body of the Rosary accordingly began to take shape into the form we've come to know today.

St. Louis de Montfort is credited as the author of some of the narratives used as meditations for each of the Mysteries. These three groups of Mysteries became the traditional way to pray the Rosary until, in 2002 , Blessed John Paul II, the Marian Pope, issued the Apostolic Letter *Rosarium Virginis Mariae*. In the letter, he proposed another set of meditations, called the Luminous Mysteries, which would help complete the chronological sequence of events in our Christian faith that are woven into the Rosary Mysteries.

The objective truth is that the structure of the Rosary as we know it today evolved between the twelfth and fifteenth centuries. It remains a collection of prayers and meditations structured around fifty Hail Marys and the gospel Mysteries revealed in scripture, and this collection has been in existence since at least the 1500s—more than five hundred years.

St. Dominic: Real Man Praying for the Church

St. Dominic, the man of church tradition and history, lived in the 1200s. History remembers him as a strong man, capable of great physical endurance, and a tireless preacher. The first great propagator of the Rosary was known as a great warrior for the fundamental truths of the faith.

At age thirty-three, young Fr. Dominic exercised his priestly ministry in southern France. As part of his priesthood, he came into contact with a dangerous heresy that threatened the Church.

It was during this time that the tradition of the Rosary comes to us. The form in which it has come down to us through time is best stated in the words of P. Cornelius de Snecka, a disciple of the French Dominican Blessed Alan de la Roche:

> We read that at the time when he was preaching to the [heretics], St. Dominic at first obtained but scanty success: and that one day, complaining of this in pious prayer to our Blessed Lady, she deigned to reply to him, saying: "Wonder not that you have obtained so little fruit by your labors, you have spent them on barren soil, not yet watered with the dew of divine grace. When God willed to renew the face of the earth, he began by sending down on it the fertilizing rain of the Angelic Salutation. Therefore preach my Psalter composed of 150 Angelic Salutations and 15 Our Fathers, and you will obtain an abundant harvest."[3]

With this new weapon, St. Dominic confronted those threatening the Church with their heresies, utilizing the Rosary Mysteries as the point of reference for remembering and understanding the faith. He traveled tirelessly beyond his native France and throughout Europe, and—armed with the Rosary as a weapon for our Church and our faith—he converted the heretics to Christianity and helped to save our Church.

That such a man, in the face of odds clearly stacked against him, would rely on a simple prayer method to combat those who would threaten the foundations of Christianity is a testament to the resolute faith and courageous virtue of the saint. Almost all of the popes who consider the origin and history of the Rosary credit him with successfully propagating the Rosary throughout Europe precisely when the Church on that continent was in danger. In the words of Pope Benedict XV, when asked about St. Dominic's connection to the Rosary,

> You ask whether St. Dominic was the first institutor of the Rosary, and show that you yourselves are bewildered and entangled in doubts on the matter. Now, what value do you attach to the testimony of so many Popes, such as Leo X (1521), Pius V (1572), Gregory XIII (1585), Sixtus V (1590), Clement VIII (1605), Alexander VII (1667), Blessed Innocent XI (1689), Clement XI (1721), Innocent XIII (1724) and others who unanimously attribute the institution of the Rosary to St. Dominic, the founder of the Dominican Order, an apostolic man who might be compared to the apostles themselves and who, undoubtedly due to the inspiration of the Holy Spirit, became the designer, the author, promoter, and most illustrious preacher of this admirable and truly heavenly instrument, the Rosary?[4]

The religious order that points to him as its founder, the Dominicans, is today considered the guardian of the Rosary. St. Dominic, whose feast day is the birth date of my own saintly mom, August 8, was clearly a "real man" whose story endures the test of time. You judge the man and his resulting spiritual acts by their fruits (cf. Mt 7:16). Surely, the fruit of the Rosary prayer within and for the Church endures.

The Battle of Lepanto

No discussion of the history of the Rosary would be complete without a description of the epic and historic Battle of Lepanto. While engaged in a protracted war with the Muslim Turks over the control of Eastern Europe and in particular the Mediterranean,

Pope Pius V organized a fleet of ships to engage the Muslim Turkish navy. Pope Pius V implored all the faithful to fervently pray the Rosary and ask our Blessed Mother to intercede on behalf of the Christians. Despite being hopelessly outnumbered in quantity of ships and fighting men, the Muslim Turks were defeated at the Battle of Lepanto on October 7, 1571.

Pope Pius V declared this day to be the Feast of the Holy Rosary and asked all to give thanks to "Our Lady of Victory" for her timely intercession in answer to the faithful's praying of the Rosary. This feast remains important in our church to this day, testifying to the Rosary's significance in our Church's history.

St. Louis de Montfort: The Apostle of the Rosary

St. Louis Marie Grignion de Montfort is remembered as the "Apostle of the Cross and the Holy Rosary." During his relatively short priesthood, he was known by many names, including "the priest with the big Rosary" and the "Good Father from Montfort." As the author of *The Secret of the Rosary* and a promoter of its power, many credit this missionary preacher as the one who modified the praying of the Rosary into the form that we know today.

Louis Marie Grignion was born in rural France in a town called Montfort on January 31, 1673. Once he became a priest, he decided to drop his surname and refer to himself by the town of his birth in order to emphasize that it was there that he was baptized into Christ Jesus. Biographies of St. Louis de Montfort, who served as a priest in the first decade of the 1700s, depict an intense and faithful man, one who engaged his personal inner struggles with an almost extreme discipline and devotion. He relished and sought out opportunities for self-sacrifice and, in doing so, sought to ensure that he did not grow too soft or comfortable—neither in his faith nor in his life as a man. He accepted and embraced the crosses given to him by life as opportunities to grow in holiness.

This approach to life began with Louis's initial journey to the priesthood. For his trip to join the seminary, his loving Catholic family provided a new set of clothes and a pocketful of money to ensure that he had the basics with which to safely and comfortably travel from Montfort to Paris. History records that he was barely out of town before he exchanged his new clothes for those of a beggar and gave away the money to the poor and needy he encountered. This self-deprivation, his almost heroic humility, typified Louis's approach to his own life. His own comfort, his own earthly existence was unimportant, almost a nuisance. What was paramount to him was preaching the good news at the service of our Blessed Mother. He felt called to be a missionary preacher, especially an international traveling missionary. In the end, he never traveled outside his native France, but one of the lessons of his life is that if we persevere, we can serve as effective missionaries to our own people.

The Rosary occupied a significant place in Fr. Louis de Montfort's spiritual life and in the way that he executed his vocation. He loved preaching about "secrets." He saw the Rosary as a wonderfully secret way of knowing and loving Mary and then getting intimately closer to Jesus through her. Therein exists perhaps the biggest "secret" of this itinerant preacher: to Jesus through Mary through the Rosary.

The influence of Fr. Louis's relatively short priesthood in rural France and his love of the Rosary is often remembered in the matter of the Calvary at Pontchâteau in western France. When he announced his determination to build a Calvary on a neighboring hill in Pontchâteau, the idea was enthusiastically received by the locals. For fifteen long months, hundreds and hundreds of peasants, upper-class farmers, and pilgrims joined and prayed together in a spirit of devotion to make the priest with the big Rosary's vision a reality.

From large pillars surrounding the summit of the Calvary, "an enormous Rosary with beads as big as medium-sized cannonballs" hung.[5] At the foot of the mountain, surrounding the

monument, Fr. Louis planted 150 fir trees at an equal distance
from one another, symbolizing the 150 Hail Marys of the Rosary.
Interspersed between every ten fir trees, a cypress tree was
planted, representing the Our Father. This living Rosary would
would not be complete without the Mysteries—those points of
faith that Fr. Louis insisted be a part of a complete praying of
the Rosary. Fr. Louis also intended to build fifteen chapels to
house life-sized representations of the Mysteries of the Rosary.

When the project was finally completed, a royal decree by
King Louis XIV was received by the local bishop's office and
then delivered personally to Fr. Louis. The decree commanded
that the whole structure be demolished and the land restored to
its former condition. One can only imagine the typical person's
disappointment in such a development.

Fr. Louis's unwavering devotion and impatience with hyp-
ocritical folly had created many enemies for this missionary
preacher. Indeed, his enemies convinced the governor of Brit-
tany that the Calvary being built at the travelling priest's direction was instead a fortress capable of providing aid and cover to
revolutionaries. For several months thereafter, hundreds of local
peasants, guarded by a contingent of soldiers, were compelled
to painstakingly destroy this labor of love and faith. Legend
has it that Fr. Louis was not visibly disturbed on receiving this
humiliating news, exclaiming only, "Blessed be God!" Other
biographical accounts state that Fr. Louis missed the dedication
ceremonies so that he could immediately walk the long distance
to appeal directly to the bishop to save the Calvary. In either
event, Fr. Louis de Montfort's life as an Apostolic Missionary,
the title that Pope Clement XI personally bestowed upon him,
was never easy.

More than a hundred years after St. Louis de Montfort's
death, that same Calvary was rebuilt. The Good Father of Montfort's vision exists today and serves as a pilgrimage site for hundreds of thousands of faithful pilgrims to live and enjoy their
faith (see www.calvairedepontchateau.com).

Those same enemies who arranged the destruction of Fr. Louis's beloved Calvary, irritated by his uncompromising devotion and confrontational impatience with their lukewarm faith, blocked Fr. Louis's mission to a particular diocese. During a mission at La Rochelle, his enemies even poisoned his cup of broth. He swallowed the antidote quickly, but the health of this once strong and passionate man, who regularly walked the countryside of France in service of his vocation, was chronically impaired from that day forward.

Worn out by hard work and the chronic sickness, Fr. Louis finally came to Saint-Laurent-sur-Sèvre in April 1716 to begin his final mission. The priest with the big Rosary fell ill and died at Saint-Laurent-sur-Sèvre on April 28, 1716. He was only forty-three years old and had been a priest for just sixteen years.

Nevertheless, Fr. Louis de Montfort influenced the teaching and spirituality of the entire Church for more than two centuries. It is no surprise that the popes with a special devotion to the Rosary and to our Blessed Mother most actively advanced his cause for sainthood. Pope Leo XIII, the "Pope of the Rosary," beatified him in 1888. Pope Pius XII, also an avid promoter of the Rosary, canonized Louis Marie Grignion de Montfort on July 27, 1947. The future Pope John XXIII, then a papal nuncio, presided over a celebration at the Calvary of Pontechâteau in June 1948 with 200,000 devotees of Fr. Louis de Montfort to commemorate his canonization.

Three religious congregations trace their foundation to St. Louis de Montfort: the Daughters of Wisdom, the Company of Mary (the order of "Montfort Priests"), and the Brothers of Saint Gabriel (the teaching order). The Company of Mary, built with Fr. Louis's influence, serves today in the dioceses of Brooklyn, Rockville Centre, Hartford, and Saint Louis and as missionaries in Nicaragua and several other coutries throughout the world. A priest of the Company of Mary Fr. Hugh Gillespie S.S.M., has personally served as an important part of my growth and deepening conversion through my own "Total Consecration" to Jesus through Mary and my studies in Montfort spirituality. So, in effect, Fr. Louis has had a direct influence on my own life.

St. Louis de Monfort's book *The Secret of the Rosary* has touched generations of devoted Christians. Fr. Louis knew that if people prayed the Rosary, they were much more fervent in their faith, so he firmly established the devotion wherever he preached. *The Secret of the Rosary* remains an enduring lesson in faith to all Christians. St. Louis de Montfort taught that "the Rosary is a priceless treasure which is inspired by God." He saw the Rosary as a way of converting even the most hardened sinners to a love of our Blessed Mother. Through her, then, they could love like Jesus loved. This "secret way" is described in *The Secret of the Rosary* and also in two of his other works: *The Secret of Mary* and *Treatise on True Devotion to the Blessed Virgin Mary*.

This last work, *Treatise on True Devotion to the Blessed Virgin Mary*, continues to profoundly change lives today. It calls on us to serve as "loving slaves" of Jesus through a Total Consecration of ourselves to Jesus through Mary. Fr. Karol Wojtyla, later Pope (now Blessed) John Paul II, said that reading *Treatise on True Devotion to the Blessed Virgin Mary* was "a turning point in my life." He adopted as his papal motto the words *Totus Tuus*, St. Louis de Montfort's short form of consecration, which essentially means "all for Jesus through Mary."

St. Louis Marie Grignion de Montfort's "secrets" establish him as a "real man" in the history of the Rosary.

Pope Leo XIII: The Pope of the Rosary

Pope Leo XIII was the leader of our Church during difficult times. He describes the period as follows:

> Now, Venerable Brethren, you know the times in which we live; they are scarcely less deplorable for the Christian religion than the worst days, which in time past were most full of misery to the Church. We see faith, the root of all the Christian virtues, lessening in many souls; we see charity

growing cold; the young generation daily growing in depravity of morals and views; the Church of Jesus Christ attacked on every side by open force or by craft; a relentless war waged against the Sovereign Pontiff; and the very foundations of religion undermined with a boldness which waxes daily in intensity. These things are, indeed, so much a matter of notoriety that it is needless for Us to expatiate on the depths to which society has sunk in these days, or on the designs which now agitate the minds of men. (*QP*, 1)

Pope Leo XIII stood as the leader of the entire Catholic Church, as the successor to St. Peter during these "distressing times," yet he chose the same tool to lead his Church and its faithful as did those "real men" of the past who faced difficult times: the Rosary. Over the course of his papacy, Pope Leo XIII wrote eleven different encyclicals with the Rosary as the subject. He added the title "Queen of the Rosary" to the Church's Litany of Loreto, declared October as the month of the Rosary, and became the tireless promoter of the Rosary at the start of the Industrial Revolution—a time in which mankind began to rely more and more on itself and less and less on God and Christian faith.

In reading those encyclicals, I am struck by how confident, how certain Pope Leo XIII was that the Rosary was *the* answer. There was no question in his mind that the Rosary would be the solution to the challenges faced by the Church. He knew that the Rosary nourished the faith in a way that few other things could. He knew that the Rosary "fosters a spirit of piety" and that in the Rosary we find "an unexcelled form of prayer, an instrument well adapted to preserve the faith and an illustrious example of perfect virtue, [which] should be often in the hands of the true Christian and be devoutly recited and meditated upon" (*MDM, 29*).

Pope Leo XIII's advocacy of perseverance in prayer stands as his greatest message, and his devotion to the Rosary provides a clear sign that real men pray the Rosary.

The Rosary: A Timeless Tool for Real Men

Although we cannot fully grasp the details of an eternal God, as our faith grows, we begin to know that somehow God does indeed exist beyond space and time. That reality becomes comforting and uniting and exciting. Praying the Rosary becomes a way through which we transcend geography and time and grow in faith.

Prayer is to raise our hearts and minds to God. When we do so, we join in that community of believers that has done the same—at different times in history and all over our world. When we pray the Rosary today, we plug directly into that timelessness. We pray with Mary, alongside those people whom St. Dominic was evangelizing, and with those same illiterate farmers who longed to experience the peaceful tranquility of the monks and to commune in prayer with our God.

Those faithful believers many years ago prayed the same prayers that we do. They used the words that Jesus gave us in the Gospels of Luke and Matthew: the Our Father. They used the same words that the Angel Gabriel, the messenger of God, used to address our Blessed Mother: "Hail, full of grace." The faithful reflected on those same incredible, transformative moments in the life and teachings of Jesus and Mary that we now call the Rosary Mysteries.

My "Saul conversion moment"—praying the Rosary in tears amid the pre-dawn mist in the Marian prayer garden of that beautiful, sacred, and isolated monastery—transported me outside myself in some inexplicable way to that transcendent reality. At that moment, praying the Rosary in that setting, I knew that I was somehow praying the Rosary with my mom, my grandmother, and with everyone who had ever prayed the Rosary in ecstatic prayerful communion with God.

Later, as I learned about the history of the Rosary, it made sense that every time we recite those beautiful familiar prayers, we are reciting the same words, invoking the same hopes and dreams of countless others since Jesus' time on earth. If God can transcend time and space, certainly our communications with him can and must do the same. Our prayers do indeed unite us with the entire community of faithful who have found this devotion a powerful tool for finding God. That transcendence can be a source of tremendous confidence and has the power to fortify the faith in a way that few other things can.

We can tap into that well-founded confidence by remembering those monumental occasions in the Rosary's history described previously. We know that in the fifteenth century, our pope was calling on faithful Christians to pray the Rosary for victory over the hordes who were attacking the Church. We remember that— as those thirteen British colonies were just beginning to express the beginnings of independence across the Atlantic from Great Britain—Fr. Louis de Montfort was inspiring hundreds of French peasants and nobility to build, stone by stone, a life-sized Rosary at the foot of a mountain in rural France. And as the United States of America was recovering from the war that almost tore the nation apart, Pope Leo XIII affirmatively and confidently reminded the Church that "the Rosary is the most efficacious of all prayers. . . . Indeed, it is the perfect prayer." Fast-forwarding to the twentieth century, we recall that Pope John Paul II reminded us that the Rosary is one of the most effective and powerful prayers we can pray to navigate the difficulties we face daily.

There is no magic within the body of the Rosary itself, within its metal chain or string and its beads or knots. Rather, the humble and unshakable affirmation of faith that reflecting upon those Mysteries evokes in the person praying provides the spark of faith. It is the devotion that follows from a pious recitation of these familiar prayers and the prayerful meditation upon the central Mysteries of our Christian faith that comprise both the history and the universal power of the Most Holy Rosary of the

Blessed Virgin Mary. It is the best tool to teach and lead us to perseverance in prayer.

History shows us unequivocally that real men have always prayed the Rosary.

THE TOOL BOX: SIMPLE EXERCISES TO JUMP-START PRAYING THE ROSARY

How do *you* deal with difficult things in your life? Do you ignore difficulties and hope they will go away? Do you avoid them at all costs? Do you cling to unhealthy habits or run to people with unhealthy lifestyles as a way of avoiding such difficulties?

1. Pray one decade of the Rosary by yourself. Ask our Blessed Mother to pray for you to have strength, like St. Dominic and St. Louis de Montfort, to deal with the difficult challenges you face in your life.

2. Wait a minute. How about even praying to be more like a "saint"? Is that too much to ask?

3. Go online (rmptr.org) to determine the Rosary Mysteries of the day. Meditate on those today. What are they saying to you in your life right now?

CHAPTER 4

HOW TO PRAY THE ROSARY: THE PRAYERS

> One of the principal benefits of the Rosary is to provide the Christian with a short and easy way of nourishing his faith and of preserving it from ignorance and the danger of error. . . . When faith is exercised by repeated vocal prayers, or better still, by meditating on the Mysteries, it is evidence of how close we are brought to Mary. . . . We recall to mind the wonderful work of our salvation.
>
> —Pope Leo XIII, *JS*

> This prayer, being both vocal and mental—the meditation of the principal Mysteries of religion accompanied by the recitation of five Our Fathers and five decades of Hail Marys—is wonderfully adapted to fostering devotion and promoting the practice of virtue.
>
> —Pope Benedict XV, *DAP*

As stated earlier, the Rosary has a body and a soul. The traditional prayers of the Rosary—the Our Father, the Hail Mary, the Glory Be, the Apostles' Creed, and the Hail Holy Queen—are its body. The Mysteries, those twenty salient points in the life and teachings of Jesus and Mary derived from scripture, compose its soul.

We have looked at how devoted prayer with the Rosary can produce transformational effects in knuckleheads like me and even instill confidence in popes and saints throughout history. In this chapter, we begin to examine the Rosary itself. We take each prayer, one by one, and briefly examine its content and its source.

As we arm ourselves with the knowledge of how to pray the Rosary, let us first explore the body of the Rosary through its prayers.

Because the Rosary is first and foremost a Christ-centered prayer, it must begin and end with Christ as represented through the crucifix. Accordingly, the Rosary always begins and ends with the short opening and closing prayer known well to all Catholic Christians that involves praying in the name of the Holy Trinity through the Sign of the Cross.

The remaining prayers of the Rosary include the following:

The Apostles' Creed

> I believe in God,
> the Father almighty,
> Creator of heaven and earth,
> and in Jesus Christ, his only Son, our Lord,
> who was conceived by the Holy Spirit,
> born of the Virgin Mary,
> suffered under Pontius Pilate,
> was crucified, died and was buried;
> he descended into hell;
> on the third day he rose again from the dead;
> he ascended into heaven,
> and is seated at the right hand of God the Father almighty;
> from there he will come to judge the living and the dead.
>
> I believe in the Holy Spirit,
> the holy catholic Church,
> the communion of saints,
> the forgiveness of sins,
> the resurrection of the body,
> and life everlasting. Amen.

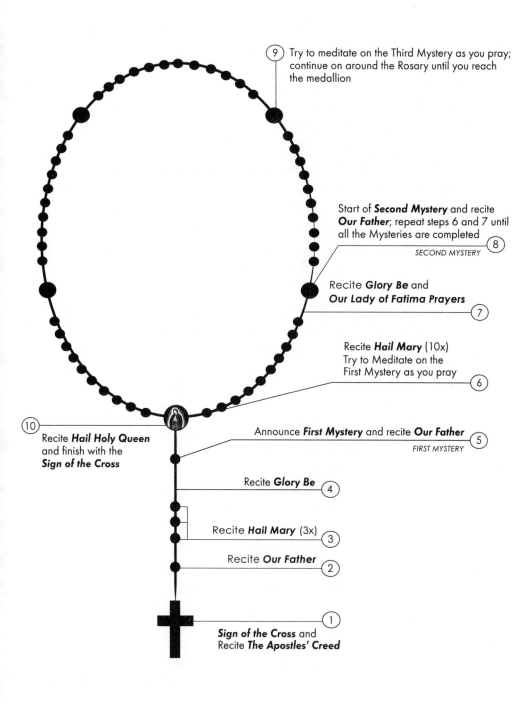

9 Try to meditate on the Third Mystery as you pray; continue on around the Rosary until you reach the medallion

Start of **Second Mystery** and recite **Our Father**; repeat steps 6 and 7 until all the Mysteries are completed

SECOND MYSTERY

8

Recite **Glory Be** and **Our Lady of Fatima Prayers**

7

Recite **Hail Mary** (10x) Try to Meditate on the First Mystery as you pray

6

10 Recite **Hail Holy Queen** and finish with the **Sign of the Cross**

Announce **First Mystery** and recite **Our Father**

FIRST MYSTERY

5

Recite **Glory Be**

4

Recite **Hail Mary** (3x)

3

Recite **Our Father**

2

Sign of the Cross and Recite **The Apostles' Creed**

1

This prayer is the ultimate profession of faith. With this prayer, we reaffirm the basic tenets of our Christianity because ultimately, to believe "in God the Father almighty," "in Jesus Christ, his only Son, our Lord," and "in the Holy Spirit" is to believe in the Trinity: God as three persons. To be a Christian is to share in that fundamental belief and to live accordingly, striving to participate fully in his life.

According to tradition, the Apostles' Creed is attributed to the twelve Apostles themselves. The prayer is composed of twelve basic statements, with each Apostle contributing one basic statement to the prayer. This origin cannot be confirmed because very few things emanating from the time of Christ were documented in writing, but oral tradition attributes authorship of this prayer to the original Twelve.

Whatever its origin or authorship, this profession of faith serves to initiate Christ-centered prayer and thus constitutes an appropriate way to begin any conversation with our Lord.

Our Father, or the Lord's Prayer

Our Father
who art in heaven,
hallowed be thy name.
Thy kingdom come;
thy will be done on earth as it is in heaven.
Give us this day our daily bread
and forgive us our trespasses
as we forgive those who trespass against us.
And lead us not into temptation,
but deliver us from evil.
Amen.

Imagine if Jesus Christ was sitting next to us in our living rooms. We would be flooded with questions, and we would listen intently to everything he had to share with us. As a result, we would probably humbly and obediently comply with his every request and strictly follow his advice to us.

That scene has already played out. Not in our living rooms, but a record exists of a conversation in which one of his disciples asks, "Lord, teach us how to pray." Jesus answered the question very directly and taught us all precisely how to pray with the text of this seminal prayer. He responds to the question unequivocally, "This is how you are to pray" (Lk 11:1–4; Mt 6:9–16).

Referred to as the "Lord's Prayer," it is truly also *our* prayer. Jesus taught us how to pray, not only by example but also directly with the exact words. As Blessed John Paul II wrote, "Jesus always leads us to the Father, for as he rests in the Father's bosom, he is continually turned toward him. He wants us to share in his intimacy with the Father, so that we can say with him: 'Abba, Father'" (*RVM*, 32).

Hail Mary, or the Angelic Salutation

> Hail Mary, full of grace,
> the Lord is with thee.
> Blessed art thou among women
> and blessed is the fruit of thy womb, Jesus.
> Holy Mary, Mother of God,
> pray for us sinners now
> and at the hour of our death. Amen.

The Angelic Salutation, as this prayer is sometimes called, is derived largely from the Gospel of Luke. As St. Louis de Montfort boldly states in The Secret of the Rosary, "The greatest event in the whole history of the world was the Incarnation of the eternal Word by whom the world was redeemed and peace was restored between God and men . . . [this] was put into effect when [Mary] was greeted with the Angelic Salutation." After such a trumpeted introduction, we should examine the source of this great prayer.

If we have difficulty finding ways to speak with our Blessed Mother, the Mother of Jesus Christ, we need look no further than the words of God the Father himself. It was God's personal messenger, the Angel Gabriel, who uttered those words to Mary directly from God: "Hail, full of grace. The Lord is with thee" (Lk 1:28). This crucial message ushers in the Incarnation—Jesus' setting aside his glory to become human for our salvation. Indeed, the importance of this greeting by the angel cannot be overstated.

The Gospel of Luke also provides the second sentence in this exquisite prayer. When Mary visits her cousin to share in the miracles about which both have recently been informed, Elizabeth, touched and inspired by the same Holy Spirit that has touched Mary, greets Mary with the well-deserved and now familiar praise, "Blessed art thou among women and blessed is the fruit of thy womb" (Lk 1:42). With each Hail Mary, we simultaneously praise both Mary *and* the fruit of her womb: our Lord Jesus Christ.

Thus, the holy name of our Savior lies at the center of this beautiful prayer. The name of Jesus Christ is placed at its center, *"the hinge* as it were," so as to highlight that he is the center of gravity that cannot be overlooked. "[I]t is precisely the emphasis given to the name of Jesus and to his mystery that is the sign of a meaningful and fruitful recitation of the Rosary," said Pope John Paul II (*RVM*, 33).

In the second part of the Hail Mary prayer, the petition, we affirm what the Gospel of Luke says—that the Blessed Virgin is the Mother of God. The Gospel of Luke provides the foundation for this confirmation of Mary as the "Mother of my Lord" (Lk 1:43). By humbly requesting "Holy Mary, Mother of God, pray for us sinners, now and at the hour of our death," we invoke her uniquely privileged relationship with Christ that enables her to intercede for us. It is appropriate that we should ask Mary, with the title bestowed upon her by God, for her prayers. We entrust our petitions to her maternal assistance and intercession.

The Angelic Salutation is thus the perfect Marian prayer. When we linger with the Hail Mary, Mary becomes a place—our special garden. It is a familiar place where we invite Mary to join hands with us. With her hand tenderly intertwined with ours, we can feel intimately comfortable and secure enough to explore the Mystery of the Rosary upon which we are meditating, to gaze upon the face of her Son, or to seek solace from the darkness of our world with the Mother of God, with our mother.

St. Louis de Montfort, the "Apostle of the Rosary," was fond of saying that "through, with, and in" the Hail Mary—and with the grace of the Holy Spirit—we can reside *with* Mary in the essence of love from which to seek and achieve a lively communion with our God. Through this prayer, we love as Jesus loved his Mother.

Mary, Mother of Jesus, Mother of all of us, pray for us always.

Glory Be, or the Gloria

> Glory be to the Father
> and to the Son
> and to the Holy Spirit,
> as it was in the beginning,
> is now,
> and ever shall be,
> world without end. Amen.

This prayer affirms the Christian definition that the Trinity is the "highest point of contemplation." The glorification of the Trinity in this prayer at the end of every decade serves as a reminder that communion with the Trinity is the goal of all Christianity.

Prayer of Our Lady of Fatima, or "The Decade Prayer"

> O my Jesus, forgive us our sins, save us from the fires of hell, lead all souls to Heaven, especially those who are in most need of your mercy.

This prayer does not constitute a standard part of the Rosary prayers. Because of its origin, neither St. Dominic nor St. Louis de Montfort nor Pope Leo XIII would have prayed these words as part of the Rosary that they knew.

Nevertheless, many faithful Rosary devotees include this prayer at the end of each decade. Its origin, as described earlier, came about in the following way:

Our Blessed Mother appeared to three shepherd children in Fatima, Portugal, six times between May 13, 1917, and October 13, 1917. Our Lady of Fatima shared numerous messages with the children. Among the messages was to pray the Rosary daily, to repent and live a sacramental life, and to pray for peace.

During the third apparition, the children were given a vision of hell by Our Lady. After that vision, she gave the children the exact text of this prayer and asked that it be prayed after each decade of our daily Rosary.

Hail Holy Queen, or the Salve Regina

> Hail, holy Queen, Mother of Mercy,
> our life, our sweetness and our hope!
> To you do we cry,
> poor banished children of Eve;
> to you do we send up our sighs,
> mourning and weeping in this valley of tears.
> Turn then, O most gracious advocate,
> your eyes of mercy toward us,
> and after this exile,
> show us the blessed fruit of your womb, Jesus.
> O clement, O loving, O sweet Virgin Mary.
> V. Pray for us, O holy Mother of God.
> R. That we may be made worthy of the promises
> of Christ. Amen.

This prayer of the Rosary is prayed, according to some customs, as a way of "bursting forth in praise to the Blessed Virgin" (*RVM*, 37).

The prayer appears to date back to the 1100s, and it remains well-known today by those who pray the official prayer of the Catholic Church, the Liturgy of the Hours. Members of religious communities, those in seminary formation, many lay groups, etc., know and sing the *Salve Regina* to conclude meetings or prayers at the end of the day.

In the *Salve Regina*, we, the sinners of earth, gather with the angels and saints of heaven, to thank the woman who brought us Jesus Christ, the Way, the Truth, and the Life, and to ask her to graciously help us to know him, love him, and serve him as she did.

Perhaps we can identify with a quote from St. Alphonsus di Liguori's *Glories of Mary:*

> Blessed Amadeus says, "that our Queen is constantly before the Divine Majesty, interceding for us with her most powerful prayers." And as in heaven "she well knows our miseries and wants, she cannot do otherwise than have compassion on us; and thus, with the affection of a mother, moved to tenderness towards us, pitying and gentle, she is always endeavoring to help and save us."[1]

If our Lord can honor his mother, perhaps we should also because he commanded us to honor our parents as well in the fourth Commandment.

Concluding Prayer

> O God, whose only begotten Son, by whose life, death and Resurrection, has purchased for us the rewards of eternal life.
>
> Grant, we beseech thee, that by meditating upon these mysteries of the Most Holy Rosary of the Blessed Virgin Mary, that we may imitate what

they contain and obtain what they promise,
through Christ our Lord. Amen.

This prayer is used by many to conclude the Rosary. Its source is almost as old as the traditional Rosary itself. This prayer was one of those composed specifically for the Feast of Our Lady of the Rosary in 1571 to celebrate the victory at the Battle of Lepanto.

All these beautiful prayers set the table for the main course. Meditating upon the Mysteries is aided by the steady drumbeat of these central prayers. How could our Lord not be listening earnestly when we use the words that his Son himself gave us? How could our Blessed Mother not sit up and listen lovingly to our petitions when we invoke the words that changed her life and made her "blessed" for all generations? How could Mary not be pulling for us and praying with us when we use the words of the messenger of God himself?

These meaningful prayers provide the best possible as well as the most comforting and familiar environment for us to begin our journey, preferably a daily one, into the good news of the gospel Mysteries.

THE TOOL BOX: *SIMPLE EXERCISES TO JUMP-START PRAYING THE ROSARY*

1. Pray one decade of the Rosary out loud. Do any of the prayers speak to you in a special way?

2. Choose one of the prayers and think about the words, analyzing each sentence and each phrase.

3. Write one paragraph about what that prayer means to you or, if you don't like to write, explain to a child what that prayer means to you.

4. Pick one prayer that you don't know and memorize it.

5. Go buy a CD or download an audio version of the Rosary from iTunes or some other source. Pray along with the audio recording.

CHAPTER 5
HOW TO PRAY THE ROSARY: THE MYSTERIES

Blessed John Paul II called the Rosary "an exquisitely contemplative prayer" (*RVM*, 12). The Mysteries of the Rosary are twenty aspects of the life and teachings of Jesus and Mary that chronologically follow the story of our New Testament salvation. Contemplating the Rosary Mysteries means entering into prayerful thought on the meaning of the lessons that are woven into those stories, asking the Holy Spirit to reveal how they apply to our lives on any given day.

In visiting these Mysteries as part of our daily prayer life, we should never run into a situation where the Mysteries or the Rosary become stale or are somehow inapplicable. They remain dynamic and relevant even as our station in life changes. Our life is always in a state of flux. The main anchor in contemplating these Mysteries is our relationship to God. Anchoring our prayer life to contemplating these Mysteries, with Mary at our side, provides us with the stability of faith.

Praying the Rosary intentionally and in this anchoring way permits us to, as Blessed John Paul II wrote, "rediscover the Rosary . . . in the light of Scripture, in harmony with the Liturgy and in the context of our daily lives."

Pope John XXIII offered his meditations on the Mysteries of the Rosary as part of his Apostolic Letter *The Religious Convention and the Rosary*. In the letter, he offers a "sample of the devout thoughts which are to be found in every decade of the Rosary. . . . These simple and spontaneous notes may well suit the spirit of many people who really wish to overcome the monotony of simple recitation. These are useful and fitting helps toward a more intense personal devotion, a more ardent fervor of prayer for the salvation and peace of all nations" (*RCR*, I).

The following sections offer a sample of my own reflections in my daily prayer life on these Mysteries, combined with the profound meditations of Pope John XXIII to further illustrate specific points. The papal meditations that conclude each section are excerpts from *The Religious Convention and the Rosary*. Together, they represent the range of depth and beauty that can be realized within our daily lives by contemplating the Rosary Mysteries—from the most pragmatic to the most profoundly theological.

Meditating on the Gospel through the Mysteries

The Rosary is an "exquisitely contemplative prayer" and should not be a "mechanical repetition of formulas." Rather, the "recitation of the Rosary calls for a quiet rhythm and a lingering pace" (*RVM*, 12).

The primary focus of praying the Rosary should be to meditate upon the life and teachings of Jesus Christ, which are summarized in the Mysteries "as seen through the eyes of her closest to the Lord" (*RVM*, 12): Mary, his mother.

The twenty Mysteries provide an "executive summary" of, or highlight, important events contained within the gospels and in scripture, which memorialize the life and teachings of Jesus Christ and Mary.

Primarily for convenience and brevity, the Mysteries may be prayed in four distinct groups: the Joyful, Sorrowful, Luminous, and Glorious Mysteries. Certain Mysteries can be focused upon during specific days of the week. For example, the Joyful Mysteries can be prayed on Mondays and Saturdays, the Sorrowful on Tuesdays and Fridays, the Luminous on Thursdays, and the Glorious on Wednesdays and Sundays. During certain times in the liturgical calendar, some, by tradition, pray only one group of Mysteries throughout that season. For example, during Advent, some pray only the Joyful Mysteries. During Lent, some pray only the Sorrowful. I say that it is "suggested" that certain Mysteries be prayed on certain days of the week because one will not find a declaration by the Magisterium or a section of canon law where this practice is mandated. They are simply suggested by tradition and custom.

Because I pray the Rosary daily, I find that I miss reflecting and living within the other Mysteries if I focus on just one group of Mysteries for an extended period of time. For example, if I focus on just the Joyful Mysteries during Advent, as some traditionally do, I find that I miss the Wedding at Cana and its rich messages to me. During Lent, if I only focus on the Sorrowful Mysteries, I miss the inspiration of Mary's openness to the messenger of God in the Annunciation.

The point of regularly visiting these Mysteries through the Rosary is to immerse ourselves in the faith, thereby nourishing it through the regular contemplation of our salvation history. We then learn over time to apply these faith-filled Mysteries to our lives. Knuckleheads like me need this daily reminder.

Each of these Mysteries represents a significant event in the life of Jesus and his mother, Mary. It is meditation upon these events and their accompanying lessons for Christians that comprises the "fruit" of the praying of the Rosary.

The Joyful Mysteries

To meditate upon the Joyful Mysteries, then, is to enter into the ultimate causes and deepest meaning of Christian joy. It is to focus on the realism of the mystery of the Incarnation and on the obscure foreshadowing of the mystery of the saving passion. Mary leads us to discover the secret of Christian joy, reminding us that Christianity is, first and foremost, *euangelion*, 'good news,' which has as its heart and its whole content the person of Jesus Christ, the Word made flesh, the one Savior of the World.

RVM, 20

Christians are in the joy business. The Joyful Mysteries invite us to peek into the hidden life of Jesus of Nazareth. They are marked by the joy radiating from the reality of God's affirmative "yes" to humanity. These mysteries begin with God reaching out to one of his special children, a virgin filled with grace who reaches back and also says "yes" to God in response. Personally, as a husband and a father, the Joyful Mysteries speak to me in a very tangible way.

Because the Joyful Mysteries are based entirely in scripture, in the following pages, each Mystery is presented with its correspondent scripture reading, followed by a short introductory explanation/reflection on each Mystery from my personal perspective, followed by a selection from *The Religious Convention and the Rosary*, an Apostolic Letter of Pope John XXIII.

First Joyful Mystery: The Annunciation

In the sixth month, the angel Gabriel was sent from God to a town of Galilee called Nazareth, to a virgin betrothed to a man named Joseph, of the house of David, and the virgin's name was Mary. And coming to her, he said, "Hail, favored one! The Lord is with you." But she was greatly troubled at what was said and pondered what sort of greeting this might be. Then the angel said to her, "Do not be afraid, Mary, for you have found favor with God. Behold, you will conceive in your womb and bear a son, and you shall name him Jesus. He will be great and will be called Son of the Most High, and the Lord God will give him the throne of David his father, and he will rule over the house of Jacob forever, and of his kingdom there will be no end." But Mary said to the angel, "How can this be, since I have no relations with a man?" And the Angel said to her in reply, "The Holy Spirit will come upon you, and the power of the Most High will overshadow you. Therefore the child to be born will be called holy, the Son of God. And behold, Elizabeth, your relative, has also conceived a son in her old age, and this is the sixth month for her who was called barren; for nothing will be impossible for God." Mary said, "Behold, I am the handmaid of the Lord. May it be done to me according to your word." Then the angel departed from her.

Luke 1:26–38; cf. CCC, 484

When I meditate prayerfully upon the first Joyful Mystery, the Annunciation, I often wonder if I am creating a safe and loving home where an angel of the Lord, the voice of God himself, would be welcome and whose voice would be heard by my wife, my children, or even myself. As I continue to meditate upon this Mystery, I wonder if I could move past my fear of the unknown and be like Mary, trusting fully in God's plan even if I don't know all the details. As men, we often want to know "What's the plan?" We have a need to know where we're headed, and we're trained to have back-up plans and to try to think our way through these issues, eliminating or at least minimizing any uncertainty. Mary didn't have that luxury. After some initial inquiry, presumably to confirm that the message was indeed divinely sent, she submitted herself entirely to him: "Let it be done to me according to your word" (Lk 1:38). In doing so, she provides the best example of why she is called the "first perfect disciple."

PAPAL MEDITATION

This is the first shining point of union between heaven and earth: the first of those events which were to be the greatest of all time.

When Mary Immaculate, the finest and most fragrant flower of all creation, said in answer to the angel's greeting: "Behold the handmaid of the Lord" (Lk 1:38) she accepted the honor of divine motherhood, which was in that moment realized within her. . . . From today onwards she will be Mother of God (*Mater Dei*) and our Mother (*mater nostra*) too.

What sublimity, what tender love in this first Mystery!

When we reflect on this we see that our chief and constant duty is to thank the Lord who deigned to come to save us and for this purpose made himself man, our brother man; he has joined us by becoming the son of a woman and by making us, at the foot of the Cross, the adopted sons of this woman. He wanted us who were the adopted sons of his Heavenly Father to be sons of his own Mother.

RCR, II: The Joyful Mysteries 1

Second Joyful Mystery: The Visitation

During those days Mary set out and traveled to the hill country in haste to a town of Judah, where she entered the house of Zechariah and greeted Elizabeth. When Elizabeth heard Mary's greeting, the infant leaped in her womb, and Elizabeth, filled with the holy Spirit, cried out in a loud voice and said, "Most blessed are you among women, and blessed is the fruit of your womb."

Luke 1:39–42; cf. CCC, 717

In the second Joyful Mystery, the Visitation, Mary visits her cousin Elizabeth and in the process brings Jesus to John the Baptist. I pray that I am, like St. Joseph, facilitating and helping in every way that I can to execute and satisfy God's plan, even if I can't see and appreciate the unseen mystery. When I pray and meditate upon the birth of Jesus, I can't help but relive the amazing joy of the birth of my own seven children, each of whom is a gift from God. I am led to pray that I live a life worthy of such blessing and responsibility. I pray that Mary finds me with sufficient vision and faith to see Jesus when he is presented to me in my daily life.

Because of Elizabeth's age and Mary's virginity, impossibility is a theme that surrounds this Mystery. The ladies gather in haste to celebrate that "nothing is impossible for God" (Lk 1:37). May this lesson of God's omnipotent generosity perpetually nourish my trust and faith in the Lord.

PAPAL MEDITATION

What gentleness and charm in this three months' visit made by Mary to her beloved cousin! Each of them is about to bear a child, but for the Virgin Mother this is the most sacred maternity that it is possible to imagine on earth. Their two songs mingle and respond in a sweet harmony, "Blessed are you among women" (Lk 1:42) on the one hand, and on the other, "God my Savior has regarded the low estate of his handmaiden: for behold, henceforth all generations will call me blessed" (Lk 1:48).

RCR, II: The Joyful Mysteries 2

Third Joyful Mystery: The Birth of Our Lord

In those days a decree went out from Caesar Augustus that the whole world should be enrolled. This was the first enrollment, when Quirinius was governor of Syria. So all went to be enrolled, each to his own town. And Joseph too went up from Galilee from the town of Nazareth to Judea, to the city of David that is called Bethlehem, because he was of the house and family of David, to be enrolled with Mary, his betrothed, who was with child. While they were there, the time came for her to have her child, and she gave birth to her first-born son. She wrapped him in swaddling clothes and laid him in a manger, because there was no room for them in the inn.

Luke 2:1–7; cf. CCC, 525

With the third Joyful Mystery, the Nativity, I find myself sharing in Mary and Joseph's joy at the birth of their newborn miracle. There are few times more special in the life of a family than when a baby is born. For a couple, their love has become manifest in a new life. Together, they will nurture, love, and raise this child so that God's will may be done. Mary and Joseph felt that same divine joy and responsibility. As I reflect upon that intimate scene, I pray to duplicate that joyous responsibility within my home—for *my* holy family. I pray that we never lose the joy of Christ's birth and that I be born again in the faith every time I delve into these Mysteries, singing "Glory to God in the highest" with the example of my life.

PAPAL MEDITATION

At the hour appointed by the laws of the human nature he had assumed, the Word of God, now made man, issues from the holy shrine, the immaculate womb of Mary. He makes his first appearance in this world in a manger: the cattle are there, chewing their straw, and all around are silence, poverty, simplicity and innocence. Angels' voices are heard in the sky, announcing peace, that peace which the new baby has brought to us. His first worshippers are Mary his mother and Joseph, thought to be his father, and after these some humble shepherds who have come down from the hills, led by angels' voices. Later on comes a caravan of distinguished persons guided from far, far away by a star; they offer precious gifts, full of a mysterious meaning. Everything that night at Bethlehem spoke a language that the whole world could understand.

Pondering this mystery every knee will bow in adoration before the crib. Everyone will look into the eyes of the divine Infant which gaze far away, almost as if he could see one by one all the peoples of the earth.

RCR, II: The Joyful Mysteries 3

Fourth Joyful Mystery: The Presentation in the Temple

When eight days were completed for his circumcision, he was named Jesus, the name given him by the angel before he was conceived in the womb. When the days were completed for their purification according to the law of Moses, they took him up to Jerusalem to present him to the Lord, just as it is written in the law of the Lord, "Every male that opens the womb shall be consecrated to the Lord," and to offer the sacrifice of "a pair of turtledoves or two young pigeons," in accordance with the dictate in the law of the Lord.

Luke 2:21–24; cf. CCC, 527

When I pray upon the Presentation, or the fourth Joyful Mystery, I feel the weight of my responsibility to raise my children in the faith. Joseph and Mary fully and dutifully complied with Mosaic law and presented their child in the Temple. In doing so, they touched the lives of two people, Simeon and Anna, who had been waiting to see the Messiah. As I comply with my responsibility to "present" my children to God through our church, I pray that their lives and the lives within his Church may fully and dutifully satisfy the law of Jesus. I pray for the wisdom and faith of Simeon so that when the Lord is presented to me in my daily journey, I may recognize him—even in unexpected places.

PAPAL MEDITATION

Jesus carried in his mother's arms, is offered to the priest, to whom he holds out his arms: it is the meeting, the contact of the two Covenants. He is already the "light for revelation to the Gentiles" (Lk 2:32), he, the splendor of the chosen people, the son of Mary. St. Joseph also is there to present him, an equal sharer in this rite of legal offerings according to the law.

This child is the "light for revelation to the Gentiles" (Lk 2:32), and the glory of the chosen people.

RCR, II: The Joyful Mysteries 4

Fifth Joyful Mystery: The Finding of Jesus in the Temple

Each year his parents went to Jerusalem for the feast of Passover, and when he was twelve years old, they went up according to festival custom. After they had completed its days, as they were returning, the boy Jesus remained behind in Jerusalem, but his parents did not know it. Thinking that he was in the caravan, they journeyed for a day and looked for him among their relatives and acquaintances, but not finding him, they returned to Jerusalem to look for him. After three days they found him in the temple, sitting in the midst of

the teachers, listening to them and asking them
questions, and all who heard him were astounded
at his understanding and his answers.

Luke 2:41–47; cf. CCC, 534

The finding of Jesus in the Temple is the fifth and final Joyful
Mystery. Reflecting upon this Mystery forces me to realize that
I must be held accountable for being a good steward of my children. I must ensure that they are never "lost" to God. As a dad,
I know that I must teach them the faith so that they will always
be "found" doing the work of the Father. As a man, I pray that
when the Lord finally calls me home, that he finds me fully and
satisfactorily accomplishing his will.

PAPAL MEDITATION

Jesus is now twelve years old. Mary and Joseph have
brought him with them to Jerusalem, for the ritual
prayers. Without warning he disappears from their sight,
although they are so watchful and so loving. Great anxiety
and a fruitless search for three days. Their sorrow is followed by the joy of finding him again, there, under the
porches of the Temple. He is speaking with the doctors
of the Law. How significant is the account given us by St.
Luke, with his careful precision! They found him then,
sitting in the midst of the doctors "listening to them and
asking them questions" (Lk 2:46).

Christ, in natural as in supernatural revelation, is
never absent; he is always in his place, in the midst: "For
you have one master, the Christ" (Mt 23:10).

RCR, II: The Joyful Mysteries 5

The Sorrowful Mysteries

> The Gospels give great prominence to the sorrowful mysteries of Christ. From the beginning, Christian piety, especially the Lenten devotion of the Way of the Cross, has focused on the individual moments of the passion, realizing that here is found the culmination of the revelation of God's love and the source of our salvation. The Rosary selects certain moments from the passion, inviting the faithful to contemplate them in their hearts and to relive them.
>
> *RVM, 22*

The Sorrowful Mysteries help me appreciate the difficult challenges that I face in life as I sit at the school of Mary and alongside Jesus himself.

First Sorrowful Mystery: The Agony in the Garden

> Then Jesus came with them to a place called Gethsemane, and he said to his disciples, "Sit here while I go over there and pray." He took along Peter and the two sons of Zebedee, and began to feel sorrow and distress. Then he said to them, "My soul is sorrowful even to death. Remain here and keep watch with me." He advanced a little and fell prostrate in prayer, saying, "My Father, if it is possible, let this cup pass from me; yet, not as I will, but as you will." When he returned to his disciples, he found them asleep.
>
> Matthew 26:36–40; cf. CCC, 2849

The agony in the garden, or the first Sorrowful Mystery, provides a concrete example of the ultimate "real man." Jesus knew what his fate was going to be, and maybe his humanity was revealed, and he was a bit concerned, perhaps even scared, of that imminent future. Jesus' response was to pray—to reach out to his Father. "When he was faced with agony; he prayed the longer," writes Pope Leo XIII (*SI*, 2). As I face my own pressing professional and daunting personal challenges, I have an example of how a real man responds: pray but with ultimate acceptance of the Lord's plan. May I not fall asleep at the task but instead be ever vigilant to watch for Jesus.

PAPAL MEDITATION

Our heart is moved as we continually return to the image of the Saviour, in the place and hour of his supreme anguish: "and his sweat became like great drops of blood falling down upon the ground" (Lk 22:44). Suffering of the innermost soul, extreme bitterness of loneliness, exhaustion of the broken body. His suffering can only be measured by the imminence of his Passion which now Jesus sees, no longer as far away, or even as near at hand, but as present in that hour.

The scene in the garden strengthens and encourages us to force all our will to an acceptance, a full acceptance, of suffering sent or permitted by God: "Not my will but thine be done" (Lk 22:42). Words which tear the heart and heal it again, for they teach us what passionate fervour the Christian can and must feel if he is to suffer with Christ who suffers, and give us the final certainty of the indescribable merits he obtained for us, the certainty of the divine life, a life which today is lived in grace and tomorrow in glory.

RCR, II: The Sorrowful Mysteries 1

Second Sorrowful Mystery: The Scourging at the Pillar

> Then Pilate took Jesus and had him scourged. And the soldiers wove a crown out of thorns and placed it on his head, and clothed him in a purple cloak, and they came to him and said, "Hail, King of the Jews!" And they struck him repeatedly.
>
> John 19:1–3; cf. CCC, 572

As I pray through the Sorrowful Mysteries, I encounter the cruelty of the Lord's scourging, or the second Sorrowful Mystery. I wonder, "To whom in my life have I been less than fully loving and kind?" I pray that when my life's "mystery" is reviewed by the Almighty Father, I will not be revealed to be part of the crowd that is inflicting pain and humiliation upon Jesus, alive in one of his children or his Church.

PAPAL MEDITATION

> There is a great lesson here for us all. We may not be called to endure a cruel martyrdom, but we are called to the exercise of constant discipline and the daily mortification of our passions. This way, a real "Way of the Cross," is our unavoidable and indispensable duty, which at times becomes even heroic in its requirements. It leads us step by step towards an ever closer resemblance to Jesus Christ and to a share in both his merits and the atonement he gained for all sins by his innocent blood. We cannot do this in any other way—not by facile enthusiasms nor by fanaticism which, even if innocent, is always harmful.
>
> RCR, II: The Sorrowful Mysteries 2

Third Sorrowful Mystery: The Crowning with Thorns

> Then the soldiers of the governor took Jesus inside the praetorium and gathered the whole cohort around him. They stripped off his clothes and threw a scarlet military cloak about him. Weaving a crown out of thorns, they placed it on his head, and a reed in his right hand. And kneeling before him, they mocked him, saying, "Hail, King of the Jews!" They spat upon him and took the reed and kept striking him on the head. And when they had mocked him, they stripped him of the cloak, dressed him in his own clothes, and led him off to crucify him.
>
> Matthew 27:27–31; cf. CCC, 616

Dignity and grace is how Jesus responded to his "crowning" with the thorns, or the third Sorrowful Mystery. I pray that as I summon the courage to live as a fully Christian man, I can emulate the Lord's dignity and grace in the face of cruelty and evil. I pray that my wife and children and all those who know me see in me a Christ-like strength, grounded in faith in the Father.

PAPAL MEDITATION

> Another useful way of thinking about this Mystery would be to consider the grave responsibilities of those who have received greater talents and are therefore bound to make them yield greater fruit, through the continual use of their faculties and intelligence. The ministry of the mind, that is the service required of those most richly endowed with intelligence, in order to be a light and guide to all others, must be undertaken with great patience, resisting all the temptations of pride, selfishness and the disintegration which is destructive.
>
> RCR, II: The Sorrowful Mysteries 3

Fourth Sorrowful Mystery: The Carrying of the Cross

> They pressed into service a passer-by, Simon, a
> Cyrenian, who was coming in from the country, the
> father of Alexander and Rufus, to carry his cross.
> They brought him to the place of Golgotha (which
> is translated Place of the Skull).
>
> Mark 15:21–22; cf. CCC, 612

How can we be of help? When I meditate upon this scene,
the carrying of the Cross, I wonder if I would be of help to our
Lord. When I've seen the opportunity to reach out a helping
hand to someone in need, I wonder if I've refused or ignored
that gift. Will I give myself the opportunity to grow in my faith,
like Simon, and help those in need, even when not asked?

PAPAL MEDITATION

> The mystery should set before our eyes a vast vision of
> poor suffering souls: orphans, old people, the sick, the
> weak, prisoners and exiles. We pray for strength for all
> these, and the consolation which alone brings hope. We
> repeat with emotion and, we must admit, with secret
> tears, "Hail, O Cross, our only hope."
>
> RCR, II: The Sorrowful Mysteries 4

Fifth Sorrowful Mystery: The Crucifixion

> When they came to the place called the Skull,
> they crucified him and the criminals there, one on
> his right, the other on his left. [Then Jesus said,
> "Father, forgive them, they know not what they
> do."] They divided his garments by casting lots.
> The people stood by and watched; the rulers,
> meanwhile, sneered at him and said, "He saved
> others, let him save himself if he is the chosen

one, the Messiah of God." Even the soldiers jeered at him. As they approached to offer him wine they called out, "If you are King of the Jews, save yourself." Above him there was an inscription that read, "This is the King of the Jews." Now one of the criminals hanging there reviled Jesus, saying, "Are you not the Messiah? Save yourself and us." The other, however, rebuking him, said in reply, "Have you no fear of God, for you are subject to the same condemnation? And indeed, we have been condemned justly, for the sentence we received corresponds to our crimes, but this man has done nothing criminal." Then he said, "Jesus, remember me when you come into your kingdom." He replied to him, "Amen, I say to you, today you will be with me in Paradise." It was now about noon and darkness came over the whole land until three in the afternoon because of an eclipse of the sun. Then the veil of the temple was torn down the middle. Jesus cried out in a loud voice, "Father, into your hands I commend my spirit"; and when he had said this, he breathed his last.

Luke 23:33–46; cf. CCC, 619

The Crucifixion is so rich with meaning, and I find myself frequently marveling at the Lord's love for us. I especially linger on the thought that while he hung there on the Cross dying, Jesus found the strength to love us enough to give us one more gift. He bequeathed to us the love of his mother. He turned to John, who represented all of us, and said: "Behold your Mother" (Jn 19:27). Jesus wanted me to love like he did. From the Cross, he passed onto me a love that I would know, to which I could easily and fully relate—the love of a mother and a son—for me to begin my journey to knowing him better. I pray that one day I become worthy of the gift of that special love between Mother and Son. I pray that I fully appreciate and understand the Lord's love and special sacrifice for us.

PAPAL MEDITATION

Life and death are the two significant and decisive elements of Christ's sacrifice. From his smile at Bethlehem, the same smile which lights up the faces of all the children of men when first they appear on earth, to his last gasp and sob on the Cross, which gathered all our sufferings into one to hallow them, and wiped away all our sins by atoning for them, we have seen how Christ lived in this our earthly life. And Mary is still there, beside the Cross, as she was beside the babe at Bethlehem. Let us pray to her, this Mother, pray to her so that she too may pray for us "now and at the hour of our death."

In this Mystery we might see foreshadowed the mystery of those who—what sadness in this thought!—will never know anything about the blood that was poured out for them too by the Son of God; and above all the mystery of obstinate sinners, of unbelievers, of those who have received, still do receive and then refuse the light of the Gospel! With this thought our prayer expands in a vast longing, in a sigh of heartfelt reparation, the longing to reach to the ends of the earth with our apostolate; and we earnestly pray that the Precious Blood, poured out for all mankind, may at long last bring to all, to all men everywhere, salvation and conversion, that the Blood of Christ may be to all the pledge and promise of eternal life.

RCR, II: The Sorrowful Mysteries 5

The Glorious Mysteries

> [The Glorious Mysteries] lead the faithful to an ever greater appreciation of their new life in Christ, lived in the heart of the Church, a life of which the scene of Pentecost itself is the great "icon." The glorious mysteries thus lead the faithful to greater hope for the eschatological goal toward which they journey as members of the pilgrim People of God in history. This can only impel them to bear courageous witness to that "good news" which gives meaning to their entire existence.
>
> RVM, 23

The Glorious Mysteries speak directly to our Christian faith. We either believe these sacred Mysteries of our faith or we do not. We are either fully Christians or not. My days of being a "cafeteria Catholic" are over. Whenever my mom called me that while she was alive, I would chuckle and accept the label as a joke. To the contrary, it was her warning to me to live fully as a Catholic Christian. I am still joyfully learning all that that vocation means.

First Glorious Mystery: The Resurrection

> But at daybreak on the first day of the week they took the spices they had prepared and went to the tomb. They found the stone rolled away from the tomb; but when they entered, they did not find the body of the Lord Jesus. While they were puzzling over this, behold, two men in dazzling garments appeared to them. They were terrified and bowed their faces to the ground. They said to them, "Why do you seek the living one among the dead?"
>
> Luke 24:1–5; cf. CCC, 651

In the Glorious Mystery of the Resurrection, I am often struck by the reality that it was the women, Mary Magdalene and the others, who were at the tomb first and to whom the risen Lord first revealed himself. As I meditate on that Mystery, I pray that I learn to develop the intuition and special gift of the Holy Spirit that women seem to possess, which enables them to profoundly connect to the mysteries of our faith. I know I need our Blessed Mother's help to even begin to approach that level. I pray that I may live a fully Christian life enriched by the joy of knowing that Christ kept his promises for us. He promised he would conquer death, and he did. Our God is a God who keeps his promises. May I be made worthy of the promises of Christ.

PAPAL MEDITATION

This is the mystery of death challenged and defeated. The Resurrection marks the greatest victory of Christ, and likewise the assurance of victory for the holy Catholic Church, beyond all the adversities and persecutions of past yesterdays and tomorrow's future. Christ conquers, reigns and rules.

In the splendor of this mystery we see with the eyes of faith, as living and united with the risen Jesus, the souls who were most dear to us, the souls of those who lived with us and whose sufferings we shared. How vividly the memory of our dead rises in our hearts in the light of the Resurrection of Christ! We remember and pray for them in the very sacrifice of our crucified and risen Lord, and they still share the best part of our life, which is prayer and Jesus.

Learning to wait, trusting always to the precious promise of which the Resurrection of Jesus gives us a sure pledge—this is a foretaste of heaven.

RCR, II: The Glorious Mysteries 1

Second Glorious Mystery: The Ascension

> So then the Lord Jesus, after he spoke to them, was taken up into heaven and took his seat at the right hand of God.
>
> Mark 16:19

> While they were looking intently at the sky as he was going, suddenly two men dressed in white garments stood beside them. They said, "Men of Galilee, why are you standing there looking at the sky? This Jesus who has been taken up from you into heaven will return in the same way as you have seen him going into heaven."
>
> Acts 1:10–11; cf. CCC, 661

One lesson revealed to me in the Glorious Mystery of the Ascension is that our work for the Lord on this earth is never done. The Lord, by ascending to his rightful place, leaves us to do our part. Our job is not to "look up at the sky" but rather to live as men of faith who diligently implement that faith out of love. Jesus left this earth to resume his proper place with his Father. He left to resume the proper order. It is up to us to live a life worthy to resume our own proper place in eternal communion with our God.

PAPAL MEDITATION

> In this picture we contemplate the "consummation," that is, the final fulfillment of the promises of Jesus. It is his reply to our longing for paradise. His final return to the Father, from whom one day he came down among us in this world, is a surety for us all, to whom he has promised and prepared a place above: "I go to prepare a place for you" (Jn 14:2).

This decade of the Rosary teaches and urges us not to let ourselves be hampered by things that burden and encumber us, but to abandon ourselves instead to the will of God which draws us heavenward. As Jesus ascends into heaven to return to his Father, his arms are open to bless his first apostles, to bless all those who in the footsteps of the apostles continue to believe in him; and his blessing is in their hearts a tranquil and serene assurance of their final reunion with him and with all the redeemed, in everlasting bliss.

RCR, II: The Glorious Mysteries 2

Third Glorious Mystery: The Descent of the Holy Spirit

> When the time for Pentecost was fulfilled, they were all in one place together. And suddenly there came from the sky a noise like a strong driving wind, and it filled the entire house in which they were. Then there appeared to them tongues as of fire, which parted and came to rest on each one of them. And they were all filled with the holy Spirit and began to speak in different tongues, as the Spirit enabled them to proclaim.
>
> Acts 2:1–4; cf. CCC, 691

With Mary by our side, the Holy Spirit will be with us. Just like the disciples awaited the Holy Spirit with Mary, as a father and a husband, I feel called to create a home where Mary is present always so that the Holy Spirit will touch me, my wife, and my children, and we can live as God would have us live. Within my vocation, my job is to live a life in which the Holy Spirit is invoked and welcomed. May the Spirit fill me with the talents and abilities to reach beyond myself in service of the kingdom.

PAPAL MEDITATION

At the Last Supper the apostles received the promise of the Spirit; later, in that very room, in the absence of Jesus but in the presence of Mary, they received him as Christ's supreme gift. Indeed, what is his Spirit if not the Consoler and Giver of life to men? The Holy Spirit is continually poured out on the Church and within it every day; all ages and all men belong to the Spirit, belong to the Church. The Church's triumphs are not always externally visible, but they are always there and always rich in surprises, often in miracles.

Mary the Mother of Jesus, always our own sweet Mother, was with the apostles in the upper room for the miracle of Pentecost. Let us keep closer to her in our Rosary, all this year. Our prayers, united with hers, will renew the miracle of old. It will be like the rising of a new day, a radiant dawn for the Catholic Church, holy and growing ever more holy, Catholic and growing ever more Catholic, in these modern days.

RCR, II: The Glorious Mysteries 3

Fourth Glorious Mystery: The Assumption

For he has looked upon his handmaid's lowliness; behold, from now on will all ages call me blessed. The Mighty One has done great things for me, and holy is his name.

Luke 1:48–49

We do not want you to be unaware, brothers and sisters, about those who have fallen asleep. For if we believe that Jesus died and rose, so too will God, through Jesus, bring with him those who have fallen asleep. For the Lord himself, with a

word of command, with the voice of an archangel and with the trumpet of God, will come down from heaven, and the dead in Christ will rise first.
1 Corinthians 15:20–23; cf. *CCC*, 974

In this fourth Glorious Mystery, we are taught by the Church that Mary was "assumed" into heaven. We are taught that she was rewarded for a life of love and service to God with a graceful end to a graceful life. As I contemplate my own mortality and my eventual passing, I pray that I may look back upon a life lived "in Christ" with no regrets. I pray that, at the end, my Lord finds that I lived a sacramental life and tried to love like he loved. I know that I cannot attain such a life alone. I need Jesus to be at the center of my life to even have a fighting chance at such a fate. Holy Mary, Mother of Jesus Christ, pray for me now and at the hour of my death.

PAPAL MEDITATION

The queenly figure of Mary is illuminated and glorified in the highest dignity which a creature may attain. What grace, sweetness and solemnity in the scene of Mary's "falling asleep," as the Christians of the East imagine it! She is lying in the serene sleep of death; Jesus stands beside her, and clasps her soul, as if it were a tiny child, to his heart, to indicate the miracle of her immediate resurrection and glorification.

The Christians of the West, raising their eyes and hearts to heaven, choose to portray Mary borne body and soul to the eternal kingdom. The greatest artists saw her thus, incomparable in her divine beauty. Oh let us too go with her, borne aloft by her escort of angels!

The mystery of the Assumption brings home to us the thought of death, of our own death, and gives us a sense of serene confidence; it makes us understand and welcome the thought that the Lord will be, as we would wish him to be, near us in our last agony, to gather into his own hands our immortal soul.

RCR, II: The Glorious Mysteries 4

Fifth Glorious Mystery: The Crowning of Our Lady Queen

I have competed well; I have finished the race; I have kept the faith. From now on the crown of righteousness awaits me, which the Lord, the just judge, will award to me on that day, and not only for me, but to all who have longed for his appearance.

2 Timothy 4:7–8

And a great sign appeared in heaven, a woman clothed with the sun, with the moon under her feet, and on her head a crown of twelve stars; she was with child and she cried out in her pangs of birth, in anguish for delivery.

Revelation 12:1–2; cf. CCC, 966

In meditating upon the Crowning of Mary, I pray that I can honor Mary as Jesus himself would honor his mother—not just honoring her with external devotion but also with internal devotion, dedication, and faith. I pray that I can teach my children, by example, how to live Mary's virtues. Living and teaching her virtues by example is the best honor that I can bestow upon our Blessed Mother. I pray that the crown of righteousness be placed upon me by the Blessed Mother herself. I pray that she, on behalf of her Son, my Brother, may welcome me lovingly and assure me that I have lived a life of faith.

PAPAL MEDITATION

The great mission which began with the angel's announcement to Mary has passed like a stream of fire and light through the Mysteries in turn: God's eternal plan for our salvation has been presented to us in one scene after another, accompanying us along our way, and now it brings us back to God in the splendor of heaven.

O Mary, you are praying for us, you are always praying for us. We know it, we feel it. Oh what joy and truth, what sublime glory, in this heavenly and human interchange of sentiments, words and actions, which the Rosary always brings us: the tempering of our human afflictions, the foretaste of the peace that is not of this world, the hope of eternal life!

RCR, II: The Glorious Mysteries 5

The Luminous Mysteries

Certainly the whole mystery of Christ is a mystery of light. He is the "light of the world" (Jn 8:12). Yet this truth emerges in a special way during the years of his public life, when he proclaims the gospel of the kingdom. . . . Each of these Mysteries is a revelation of the kingdom now present in the very person of Christ. . . . In these Mysteries, the presence of Mary remains in the background. . . . Yet the role she assumed at Cana in some way accompanies Christ throughout his ministry. . . . The great maternal counsel which Mary addresses to the Church at every age, "Do whatever he tells you" (Jn 2:5) . . . is a fitting introduction to the words and signs of Christ's public ministry and it

> forms the Marian foundation of all the "Mysteries
> of light."
>
> *RVM, 22*

The Luminous Mysteries were proposed as a suggested addition to the Rosary by Pope John Paul II in his 2002 Apostolic Letter *Rosarium Virginis Mariae*. Accordingly, Pope John XXIII would not have offered his meditations upon these Mysteries in the early 1960s as we have seen with the other sets of Mysteries. Yet, these five "new" points are an integral part of the life and teachings of Jesus and Mary as reflected directly in the gospel. In fact, they are nothing "new" but are actually woven into and from our Christian faith. Any Christian can discern from them the lessons that Jesus wished to impart to us, lessons that apply to our daily lives.

The Luminous Mysteries always cause me to pause and reflect upon the fact that Jesus Christ actually walked among us. He set aside his divine glory and became physically present here on earth. I pray that, if given the chance, I would recognize him and love him no matter how he looked or what personal form he took.

First Luminous Mystery: The Baptism in the Jordan

> After Jesus was baptized, he came up from the water and behold, the heavens were opened [for him], and he saw the Spirit of God descending like a dove [and] coming upon him. And a voice came from the heavens, saying, "This is my beloved Son, with whom I am well pleased."
>
> Matthew 3:16–17; cf. *CCC*, 535

In the first Luminous Mystery, Jesus humbles himself to be baptized by John the Baptist. On one level, I appreciate the lesson that Jesus was submitting himself to God's plan. On another level, I understand that Jesus was cleansing the waters of the River Jordan for John the Baptist to then baptize us with the clean water of Jesus' sacrifice for us. I need that cleansing and am responsible for presenting that faith to my family by leading my wife and child to live a sacramental life. As a child of God, I want to please my heavenly Father. I ask for the grace to live a life that will be pleasing to our Almighty God.

Second Luminous Mystery: The Wedding Feast of Cana

> On the third day there was a wedding in Cana in Galilee, and the mother of Jesus was there. Jesus and his disciples were also invited to the wedding. When the wine ran short, the mother of Jesus said to him, "They have no wine." [And] Jesus said to her, "Woman, how does your concern affect me? My hour has not yet come." His mother said to the servers, "Do whatever he tells you." . . . Jesus told them, "Fill the jars with water." So they filled them to the brim.
>
> John 2:1–7; cf. CCC, 1613

The wedding at Cana, or the second Luminous Mystery, is my favorite Rosary Mystery. I don't know if it is problematic or appropriate to have a "favorite" Mystery, but this scene speaks to me on many different levels, depending on where I am at the moment I am contemplating it.

One of the messages of this Mystery is that of the servants fully complying with Jesus' requests. The servants filled the jars "to the brim." There is no indication that they knew Jesus, yet they fully complied with his instructions. If the servants hadn't fully complied with Jesus' directions, would the miracle have occurred? It is crucial, therefore, for me to understand and hear God's instructions and requests of me so that I, too, may fully comply. If I am going to hear that message, I need to raise my heart and mind frequently to him, and I need to ask for help to understand his directions to me. I feel a call to prayer within this Mystery. Perhaps that is Jesus' "second miracle."

Third Luminous Mystery: The Proclamation of the Kingdom of God

> This is the time of fulfillment. The kingdom of God is at hand. Repent, and believe in the gospel.
>
> Mark 1:15

> Blessed are the poor in spirit, for theirs is the kingdom of heaven. Blessed are you who mourn, for they will be comforted. Blessed are the meek, for they will inherit the land. . . . Blessed are the merciful, for they will be shown mercy
>
> Matthew 5:3–12; cf. CCC, 543

In the third Luminous Mystery, Jesus proclaimed a kingdom where our sins are forgiven. If we are to be forgiven our sins, then we certainly need to forgive others. I find myself struggling with this at times. Yet, I know that Jesus completely forgives me. I feel that mercy. I pray that I can become a better man, dare I say, a holy man so that I can fully forgive and teach my loved ones to forgive. As a man, I know that it takes strength to forgive. However, it is easy to hold a grudge. Anyone can do that. It takes a "real man" to live and forgive like Jesus teaches us.

Fourth Luminous Mystery: The Transfiguration

> After six days Jesus took Peter, James, and John his brother, and led them up a high mountain by themselves. And he was transfigured before them; his face shone like the sun and his clothes became white as light. And behold, Moses and

> Elijah appeared to them, conversing with him.
> Then Peter said to Jesus in reply, "Lord it is good
> that we are here. If you wish, I will make three
> tents here, one for you, one for Moses, and one
> for Elijah." . . . Then from the cloud came a voice
> that said, "This is my beloved Son, with whom
> I am well pleased; listen to him." . . . But Jesus
> came to them and touched them saying, "Rise
> and do not be afraid."
>
> Matthew 17:1–7; cf. *CCC*, 555

The Transfiguration reminds me that my life can be and has been transformed. Before I decided to make Jesus Christ the center of my life, I am not certain that I would have had the strength to endure the challenges I have faced and will face in the future. With my Rosary in my left hand and my crucifix in my right hand, though, I know that I am not alone. There is hope—even for knuckleheads like me—to transform ourselves into a more Christ-like future. We need not be afraid.

In this Mystery, I am also struck by how impetuous Peter is. Peter always seems willing to pipe in and eagerly offer his take on things. He seems undeterred in his desire to please Jesus, even if he doesn't always get it right. Peter's imperfections remind us of our own eagerness. We don't always get it exactly right, yet we keep trying. Peter's undaunted enthusiasm inspires me to keep trying. If this impetuous apostle can become the "rock" upon which our Church is built, as our first pope, then God can make something of me as well.

Fifth Luminous Mystery: The Institution of the Eucharist

> While they were eating, Jesus took bread, said
> the blessing, broke it, and giving it to his disciples
> said, "Take and eat; this is my body."
>
> Matthew 26:26; cf. *CCC*, 1340

Jesus wants to reach out to us through the Bible, through the Mysteries, through the Rosary, through the Eucharist. My brief studies of the Bible tell me that God has always reached out—and continues to reach out—to us. With the institution of the Eucharist, Jesus created a way to physically become a part of us again. He offers us himself as the bread of life to nourish us. He warns us that if we don't eat of his flesh and drink his blood, then we cannot share in the kingdom with him (Jn 6: 53–58). Through the Rosary, I have learned to pray that my heart may become more like Mary's heart so that when I receive the Body and Blood of Jesus, that special love between our Blessed Mother and her Son would reunite, come alive, and live within me. I pray that Jesus' grace through the Eucharist may deepen my conversion and that I one day become a real man like him.

As we consider our contemplative journey into the Rosary Mysteries, we see that these twenty points of reflection and contemplation derive from the Bible and emanate directly from our Christian faith. In these Mysteries, we invite Mary to sit with us as we visit each point of faith.

Mary herself is a part of these very Mysteries. In fact, Mary is present at the first Mystery, the Annunciation, and the last Mystery, her glorious crowning as Queen of Heaven. Her continuous presence reveals the Marian character of this Christ-centered prayer. Exploring the contours of the Mysteries shows the Rosary to be first and foremost a Christian prayer.

REAL MEN PRAY FOR WOMEN

> Even when piety and love repeat the same words
> many times, they do not for all of that repeat the
> same thing, but always express something new
> because it issues from a deep sentiment of love. . . .
> This mode of prayer breathes evangelical simplicity
> and requires humility of spirit.
>
> —Pope Pius XI, *IM*, 13

While this book is primarily for men, I have discovered that many women are drawn to, changed by, and inspired by the teachings on the Rosary that our organization, Real Men Pray the Rosary, explores. To address the Rosary more fully from a woman's perspective, my wife, Valerie, agreed to provide this chapter on how men and women can benefit mutually from the beautiful and powerful application of the Rosary to their lives.

Valerie's Story

As a wife and a mother, Real Men Pray the Rosary has had a profound impact on my life personally. As David wrote earlier, our marriage faced some very serious challenges, and I believe that it is through God's grace that we were able to overcome them and strengthen our marriage by praying, especially by praying the Rosary. As we faced those challenges, David and I focused on our personal prayer lives individually. My favorite time of the day was my morning run. Jogging outside, listening to nature all around me, and appreciating God's beautiful creation was the perfect way to pray, and the Rosary was the perfect prayer.

After many months of praying and jogging, I began to believe our Lord had a plan for our family, and the challenges we faced began to subside as I saw David's faith and earnest approach to our marriage. Our life together began to develop into a more patient, loving, and caring embrace. I believe the changes in David, particularly his devotion to ceaselessly praying the Rosary, grew through God's grace.

Through our marital challenges, the Rosary became my prayer of choice because its rhythm of prayers and meditations focused me on Christ's life and teachings. I knew that I needed Christ and his loving Mother to teach me how to become a better wife and mother.

I often meditate on Jesus' childhood with Mary and Joseph and consider how Mary responded to her husband and to those who came in contact with Jesus. Mary kept in her heart the memory of the choir of angels singing and the shepherds visiting when Jesus was born and reflected on it (Lk 2:19). When Mary and Joseph found Jesus in the Temple after they had lost him for three days, he was obedient and went home with them, and "Mary kept all these things in her heart" (Lk 2:51).

Just as Mary meditated on Jesus' life, the Rosary helps me reflect on Jesus and Mary's life as I pray, weaving my thoughts into each Hail Mary. I wonder what Mary thought when these events were taking place as Jesus was growing up. I wonder how she felt as she saw him with the crown of thorns, as he carried the Cross for our sins. How would I feel in her place? How have I felt and reacted when our children face bullying at school or some disappointment? What is Jesus teaching us through these Mysteries? As I pray the Our Father, I ask God to guide me in understanding all that his son did for us through his life and death on the Cross.

Praying the Our Father reminds me to always be forgiving and to depend on God's goodness and mercy. Through David's daily reflections on the Real Men Pray the Rosary Facebook page, various books I've read, and priests to whom we've listened,

I've learned that each Mystery has so many applications to our daily lives. Jesus taught us through word and action how to live and how to respond to challenges in our lives, and it's our responsibility to learn from him and follow him. I've also learned that I can't succeed in life on my own; only by attempting to understand and live out what Jesus and Mary teach us through their example can I begin to live a full and happy life.

Praying the Rosary in the morning grounds me and provides a pace and peace that stays with me for the rest of the day. When I pray the Rosary consistently, I've found that I'm more patient, more calm, and more thoughtful about my interactions with others. I can't help but linger on the Mysteries that I prayed in the morning as I'm cooking, cleaning, running errands, or sorting through the pile of paperwork sitting on my desk.

Mary seems to stay with me as I go about my day, and that not only encourages me to continue to pray daily, but also to share my thoughts with her throughout the day. We've all heard the phrase "What would Jesus do?" Since my re-conversion, and especially since we consecrated ourselves to Jesus through Mary, I find myself constantly asking "What would Mary do?"

As a stay-at-home mom and part-time office administrator, it's not often that I can sit still for twenty minutes or so to pray the Rosary. I usually begin the Rosary as part of our morning homeschool routine and pray a decade with our children, offering our prayer intentions and discussing the day's Mysteries. As I continue through the day, I pray a decade at a time, which allows me to reflect more on each Mystery as I'm making lunch, folding laundry, or driving to the office. I feel as though I'm reaching out to hold Mary's hand and walk with her, asking her to guide me through the day.

Being a homeschooling mom has limited my opportunity to enjoy a morning run, but I do have the privilege of praying the Rosary with our children in the morning as we begin our school day. As Jesus encouraged us to "bring the children to me," praying the Rosary with them has been a wonderful way not only to begin each day with prayer but also to discuss Jesus' life together through the Mysteries. Our children now have a good understanding of the important events in Jesus' life and the order in which they happened. They know why those events are considered sad, joyful, and glorious and how the Luminous Mysteries explain that Jesus is the Light of the World. We pray one decade and reflect on one Mystery every morning, and each day provides a wonderfully lively discussion, with each child aptly explaining the Mystery they chose to focus on and why we should meditate on it as a family. I learn so much from these discussions through our children's perspectives. They help me become more like a child in my relationship with Jesus (cf. Mt 18:3).

As we pray the Rosary as a family, we entrust into Mary's hands the intentions of our heart. Praying together offers us an opportunity to share our struggles and ask for Mary's help. The time we spend praying the Rosary together allows each of us to open our hearts to one another and share our thoughts and feelings in a way we may not otherwise be inclined to. This, in turn, strengthens us as a family.

Not too long ago, we experienced a terrible hail storm that our region had never experienced before. David had just put our youngest daughter to sleep and hadn't noticed the hail coming down outside. As he came down the stairs, he was surprised to find us all huddled together, away from any windows, praying the Rosary in our master bathroom. Somehow, our house evaded the severe damage that other homes in our area received, and our children were calm and prayerful through a frightening experience. In this time of real potential danger, our family looked to and depended on God and our Blessed Mother for protection by praying the Rosary. I am thankful that our faith continues to remain strong despite the challenges we face, and I believe praying the Rosary has fortified me—and all of us—spiritually.

Real Men Pray the Rosary Is Formed

As David's wife, I was proud to undertake the founding of Real Men Pray the Rosary, Inc., when he began discussing it with me. It really grew from his love of the Rosary, his interactions with men at church, the various ACTS retreats he served on, and his prayer life. I have no doubt that the Holy Spirit was and still is at work in our lives, as he has inspired David at his first ACTS retreat and in his efforts in RMPTR.

When David came home from an ACTS retreat team meeting in the spring of 2009 and said he wanted to form this organization, I began to understand his vision and feel his excitement. I wanted and needed to support the effort—not just because my husband was asking for my help in launching and maintaining it but also because I believed in the mission that he was about to undertake.

I believe in the truth of the statement "Real men pray." I especially believe that real men pray the Rosary.

As chief operations officer, as David called me, I did the bulk of the day-to-day work when we first formed the group since David was busy with his "day job," which he often says gets in the way of his "pray job." I loved the challenge and the opportunity to share this effort in a tangible way with David. He is very much the public part of RMPTR, and I take care of the "behind-the-scenes" work.

As we began to build the organization's formal structure, we identified some talented people who inspire us in different ways and formed a board of directors. One of our board members is Carol Vaughan. Carol and I provide the women's perspective on the RMPTR board of directors. Carol is one of the pioneers of many spiritual movements in our diocese, and she began leading classes on St. Louis de Montfort's Total Consecration more than twenty-five years ago. She now continues to work to spread the beauty of the Rosary and Total Consecration with us.

At our meetings, Carol often talks about the need for men to step up and assume a leadership role in our domestic churches, our families. That theme crystallized when I heard her say one day, almost flippantly, that we need to have "real men pray the Rosary . . . for women." It struck me that she was doubly right. That statement obviously had two meanings, both of which are incredibly important and call for real men to step up. We had been thinking of tangible ways to include women in RMPTR, especially since about half of our Facebook fans are women. As soon as I heard her say that, I knew "real men pray the Rosary for women" was the path forward.

Real Families

When thinking about the relationship between men and women, especially husbands and wives, I always think in terms of a partnership. It's not about who "wins" an argument, who is the decision-maker in the house, or who is the breadwinner. It all comes down to working together as a team, a partnership between the husband and wife, each taking on specific roles and responsibilities as they are able. For example, David—besides working to provide our financial income and undertaking many other responsibilities—is in charge of all the technology in the house, from the Wii to the computers to the televisions. It's not that I can't learn how to take care of those gadgets, but I need to spend my time taking care of other things around the house.

Given all the responsibilities David and I have, we realize that we have to divide up the duties and help each other manage our home and business and raise our children. Like most families, we work in partnership, from deciding if dinner is going to be homemade or picked up at the local deli to how we handle the issues our children face. Sometimes in the midst of our daily lives, it is easy to forget that we are a team. Praying the Rosary together provides us with a strong foundation from which to fortify our family.

If spouses work in partnership to build and sustain the family, why do we so often not take the same approach and pray with and for each other as we strive to reach our calling to become holy people? Sometimes I think we get lost in the details of life and forget the true purpose of our lives: to know, love, and serve the Lord—and, I would add, to do so *together*.

When David and I pray the Rosary together, we ask Mary to be part of our life together, part of our family. She is our heavenly Mother, on whom we depend for guidance, understanding, and grace. We ask her to pray for us through our petitions, and we pray to her in thanksgiving for our many blessings. When we take the time to pray the Rosary together, to meditate on Jesus' life, we can't help but focus our lives on following him.

Learning about Jesus through the Rosary Mysteries provides a strong example of how we are to order our relationships. Not only has it helped David and me to develop a more loving and caring relationship, but our children also see in Jesus a vivid example of how they are to grow. I remind them that Jesus was obedient to Joseph and Mary when they found him in the Temple, to Mary at the wedding at Cana, and to our heavenly Father when he was baptized in the River Jordan; and this obedience grew out of his love for his Mother and Heavenly Father. Our children have learned to turn the other cheek to those who hurt them and have also learned the importance of helping others. Most significantly, they have learned to see Jesus as their King— the one to turn to when they need help and guidance. This is a life lesson that we all learn as we grow in our understanding and love for Jesus and Mary by praying and meditating on the Rosary.

Real Men Pray the Rosary for Women

As women, living a sacramental life strengthens us spiritually, and praying the Rosary is a significant part of that. Those of us who are married need the men in our lives to live sacramentally. As part of that mutual journey toward holiness, we need men to pray that our culture accord women the dignity that we deserve. The mass-media culture objectifies women in so many ways, and more often than not, women feel the need to conform to society at large in order to be accepted and respected.

Until my husband and I grew in our Catholic faith, until we went through the process of Total Consecration to Jesus Christ through the Blessed Virgin Mary according to St. Louis de Montfort, I accepted and fell in line with many of the social norms that in many ways hurt me as a woman, but also hurt women in general. Our society often portrays women in a sexual or demeaning way. It seems like every time I turn on the television, I become more and more shocked by what I see. As I pray the Rosary and learn the heart of Mary, I'm slowly beginning to realize that concepts that I once thought were too old-fashioned and male-dominating in the Catholic faith actually are empowering to women and help preserve their dignity, modesty, and self-worth. Talking to Mary and praying with her as I pray the Rosary plants in me the seeds of her virtues: humility, faith, obedience, unceasing prayer, self-denial, purity, love, patience, kindness, and wisdom.[1] God chose Mary to be the Mother of Jesus, and as my relationship with her grows, so does my desire to model her virtues so that Jesus may also live in me.

Women need the prayerful support of their men. As basic as that notion sounds, it bears emphasizing. Women need men to encourage them as the beautifully unique and intelligent individuals God created them to be, just as men need women to support and encourage them.

Men can help address this need by praying the Rosary, growing in holiness, and praying that society may promote more positive and respectful images of women. As men, they pray that their wives, daughters, and sisters be afforded the dignity that they deserve as daughters of Christ. On this path, we witness women grow in the mold of our Blessed Mother. Attitudes change, and together, as a Body of Christ, we can do our part to create a society that encourages a truer sense of self-respect.

Total Consecration, Together

Total Consecration to Jesus Christ through Mary according to St. Louis de Montfort is a thirty-three-day process that prepares us spiritually to reaffirm baptismal vows. An important part of the consecration process is praying the Rosary. As we pray the Rosary, we learn from Jesus and Mary and conform our lives to theirs by meditating on their lives. As St. Louis de Montfort explains, Jesus came into this world through Mary, and it is through Mary that we should go to him.[2]

David and I have consecrated both our marriage and our children to Jesus and Mary. That means we put everything in Jesus' hands, through Mary, and trust that they will take care of us. David and I renew our consecration at least once a year. It is a beautiful exercise that guides us through a process of honest self-analysis and spiritual growth. Each time I undertake the consecration process, it touches my heart in a new way that reflects the state of my life at that time. As we strive toward holiness, we continue to fall into our sinful ways, but renewing our baptismal vows through this process helps keep us on track spiritually.

Men and Women Practicing Mary's Virtues

St. Louis de Montfort writes a beautiful description of Mary's virtues in his *Treatise on True Devotion to the Blessed Virgin Mary*: "Her ten principal virtues are deep humility, lively faith, blind obedience, unceasing prayer, constant self-denial, surpassing purity, ardent love, heroic patience, angelic kindness and heavenly wisdom."[3] As women, we can begin to practice one or more of these virtues daily, or we focus on a specific virtue throughout a week and see how it transforms our lives. These virtues of Mary are also solidly Christ-like virtues. They are not "female virtues," nor is there anything uniquely feminine about the strength of character that is required to practice them in today's society.

I have seen firsthand that when women live Mary's virtues, *real* men respond. Women can live Mary's virtues by meeting chauvinism with ardent charity and by meeting intransigence with heroic patience. We can do it by meeting materialism with unceasing prayer and by meeting selfishness with constant self-denial. In short, when we meet our own shortcomings and those of the men in our lives by being a living Mary to them, they will respond, "*Ave Maria.*"

Real Women Pray for Men

Real Men Pray the Rosary for Women, a group I was led to develop, has become an avenue for women to pray for men. So often women ask David and me, "How can I get my husband/son to go to church with me?" or "How can I encourage my husband to pray?" These are such simple requests from women, yet it can be so hard to find the right approach with their husbands, sons, fathers, brothers, and friends. As Doug Barry, cohost of EWTN's *Life on the Rock* and RMPTR advisory board member, said at a Women's Conference that RMPTR hosted, it's too easy for men to shrug off these requests from women and complain that they are nagging them.

So what is the answer? Doug strongly encouraged women to pray for the men in their lives. It's so simple yet so important. He followed up by urging women to gently encourage men to lead prayers at dinner or other family occasions.

In addition to praying for men, I also encourage women to consecrate their husbands and children to Jesus and the Virgin Mary, asking that the men in their families be lead to Jesus, even if they may not be ready just yet. As you pray the Rosary, Mary will prepare the men in your family and mold them through your prayers and hers. She will lead them to Jesus, her loving son.

I oftentimes find myself saying or thinking things like, "Blessed Mother, please help me be patient with my son" or "David is under so much stress at the office; please be with him and comfort him." With our teenagers, David and I often ask Jesus to show them his love and move their hearts to be closer to his. I have come to depend on Jesus and Mary so much. As I learn more about what it means to consecrate myself and my family to them, I think that just depending on them, asking them for help, and trusting in Mary's prayers is what consecrating our family to Jesus and Mary really is.

Mary joins her prayers with ours with faith that Jesus will respond. It's such a beautiful feeling to feel as though I don't have to get through the hard times on my own. My faith hasn't always been so strong, and it has only been through personal struggles, consistent prayer, and trust in God's grace that I have begun to feel, as St. Paul proclaims, that it is not I who live but God who lives in me (cf. Gal 2:20).

The Blessing That Is Our Facebook Page

One of the things that has surprised David and me is the popularity of the Facebook page that David created and maintains. The RMPTR Facebook page has generated tens of thousands of "likes," or fans of the page. The growth has been steady. Surprisingly, a full forty percent of those who have liked our page are women. Many who post their own reflections or reactions to the daily Rosary meditations are women.

In our organization and on our Facebook page, women are an integral and active part of RMPTR. I believe that women see these gestures as a way to encourage men to pray in general, and specifically to pray the Rosary. Their involvement in RMPTR is a tangible way to pray for men and to encourage their spiritual growth.

Fathers Praying the Rosary

As women, we need our fathers. We need responsible dads. We need them whether we are six months old, six years old or sixty-six years old. We need them to advise us, to encourage us, to pray for us, to support us, and—most of all—to love us.

When I first met David, I was impressed with how proud he was of being a father and how determined he was to be an *active* father in his children's lives despite the challenges of his divorce. David fought to remain a strong influence and role model in their lives. He coached their sports teams, took them to and from school whenever he had them, and relished his time with them.

I loved seeing that fatherly pride in him and admired him for it. I cherish his strong relationship with all seven of his children.

Praying the Rosary is central in David's life as a father. That centrality is reflected in the song "My Daddy Prayed" by Michele Galvan, a friend I met in consecration classes. Her lyrics beautifully illustrate the importance of fathers like David, the praying men we rely on to lead families in prayer:

MY DADDY PRAYED

> Off to school a hundred miles away, I was young, and didn't want to stay,
> but I knew as I drove away, my daddy prayed.
> Bead by bead, prayer by prayer, my daddy showed me you are there,
> and with your mercy and His love, I was led to the Lord above.
> It was time for baby to come, to the hospital, I had to run, and I knew as I drove away,
> my daddy prayed. Daddy prayed.
> As I kiss my little one each night, I know You're there, to make things right.
> You'll protect him as I walk away, because I pray.
> My daddy prayed. Daddy prayed.

"When a daddy prays," Michele Galvan explains,

> he tends to raise children of good moral character, who know what it means to be Christian. They in turn tend to pray themselves and later pray for and with their own children. There is something very beautiful about a man who prays the Rosary. By inviting Mary's intercessions and allowing her to draw him closer to her Son, he shows a willingness to lead his family with love and humility, modeling the same virtues Mary did. In today's society as our men constantly fight against the

"spirit of the world," the Rosary can be a daddy's most important weapon.

We can foster and support the role of the man or father as the spiritual "head" of the family. Not only is this divine role biblically based, it is also practical. All of us are called to a vocation, be it married, single, or consecrated religious. We should pray that the men in our lives pray about and follow their calling. Women and men together can pray for holy priests, holy consecrated religious brothers, holy single men, holy married men, and holy fathers. No matter what our vocation in life, we are called to be holy and to pray for the holiness of others in our lives.

How Real Women Can Support Real Men

Praying the Rosary supports our brothers, husbands, sons, and friends and is undoubtedly the best thing that we can do for them. Here are some other suggestions for supporting the men in our lives:

- Give men their role at the head of your domestic church.
  o Ask them to lead prayer before meals.
  o Ask them to pray at night with the children.

- Listen to music of praise and worship. Expose men to positive and prayerful music.

- Gently and lovingly encourage them to be involved in movements such as ACTS or other men's faith groups at church.

- Give them books on male spirituality; e-mail them blog posts or websites that can inspire and encourage them to strengthen their prayer life.

- Talk. It's important to work on your own faith and talk to the men in your life about it. When I am excited about my faith, my husband becomes excited, too.

THE WOMEN'S TOOL BOX: *SIMPLE EXERCISES TO JUMP-START PRAYING THE ROSARY*

1. Pray one decade of the Rosary and meditate on one Mystery every day for a week (Monday, the Joyful Mysteries; Tuesday the Sorrowful Mysteries, etc.).

2. Focus on one of Mary's virtues and try to live it for one day or one week. Choose from humility, faith, obedience, prayer, self-denial, purity, love, patience, kindness, and wisdom.

3. Pray to the Virgin Mary and ask her to pray for your husband, father, son, brother, etc.

4. If you are married, ask your husband to pray the Rosary with you. Start with praying one decade together and over time work toward praying a complete Rosary of five decades.

5. If you have children, pray a decade of the Rosary with them and determine which Mystery to meditate on as a group. Discuss the five Mysteries of the day as you decide together.

6. Learn more about the process of Consecration to Jesus through the Blessed Virgin Mary according to St. Louis de Montfort.

7. Find a consecration class you can attend or join the Real Men Pray the Rosary online consecration process based on Fr. Hugh Gillespie's book *Preparation for Total Consecration to Jesus Christ through Mary According to St. Louis de Montfort.*

THE REAL MEN PRAY THE ROSARY CHALLENGE

We've reviewed the mechanics of how to pray the Rosary, how to fit praying the Rosary into our daily life, and the timelessness of the Rosary and its importance throughout the history of the Church. Now is the time to actually begin praying the Rosary and, more importantly, integrating the Rosary into your daily life. To that end, Real Men Pray the Rosary has launched the RMPTR Thirty-Three-Day Challenge!

The challenge is simple. Using chapters 4 and 5 of this book and our Rosary pamphlet (available at realmenpraytherosary .org) as a guide, pray the Rosary every day. Stay with it for thirty-three days.

You can use any method of praying you'd like. You can pray by yourself. You can invite others to read the book with you and undertake the challenge. Maybe you can even go on a social media site, such as Facebook or Twitter, and recruit others to join you. Pray it while you run or exercise. Just pray it.

As you do, meditate upon the Mysteries with a particular emphasis on learning to apply those faith lessons to your daily life. Follow the daily Mysteries in the order that is suggested. Keep us apprised of your progress, if you'd like, on Facebook or at our website (realmenpraytherosary.org). We'll be there for support and so will the entire global RMPTR community.

Just think: for thirty-three days, you're going to be hanging around Jesus and Mary for at least twenty-five minutes a day. That just *has* to be good for you. "Just as two friends, frequently in each other's company, tend to develop similar habits, so too, by holding familiar converse with Jesus and the Blessed Virgin"

(*RVM,* 15), we can become similar to them and can learn from them.

There is a Spanish saying *"Dime con quién andas y te diré quién eres"*; it means that you can tell a lot about someone from the type of people they hang around. We all know people who are basically good people, but they just couldn't break out of the "old neighborhood," or they started hanging out with bad people and started doing bad things. Here is your chance to spend time with Jesus and Mary and do yourself a world of good. Break out of the old neighborhood.

With that as the background, we invite you to hang out with Jesus and Mary for twenty-five minutes a day and undertake the challenge by praying the Rosary daily for thirty-three days. Instead of adopting bad habits, let Jesus and Mary's habits and virtues rub off on you.

After Thirty-Three Days

If after thirty-three days of praying the Rosary daily, you *don't* feel the Holy Spirit energizing your prayer life, I want to hear from you. If you don't find yourself better able to cope with the challenges of the world with a sense of hope and tranquility, contact me directly. If it doesn't make a difference at all to you, then e-mail me at david@rmptr.org and tell me, "David, you're crazy. I didn't feel a thing." If that e-mail comes to me, we will place your name on the RMPTR website and pray for your intentions. Your name will remain there until you tell us that the Rosary has made a difference in your spiritual journey.

If, however, at the end of thirty-three days of praying the Rosary daily, you *do* feel a difference, pray it forward. If praying the Rosary every day has made a positive change in your spiritual life and has brought you closer to understanding the application of the gospel message to your daily struggles, then share the journey with someone else by praying the Rosary with a loved one. Pray with your wife. Pray with your dad. Pray with your children. Pray it forward.

Why a thirty-three-day challenge and not a thirty-day challenge? Frankly, a thirty-day challenge rings like a call to lose weight, compare price savings on coffee machines, or some other sort of marketing ploy. Thirty-three is a symbolic number. Tradition holds that the Lord Jesus lived among us for thirty-three years before his saving death and Resurrection, so a time of thirty-three days represents the fullness of his life in which we long to fully share.

This thirty-three-day challenge and journey has the full symbolic support of the fullness of our Lord's life as our ultimate destiny. And, by virtue of the Rosary, we invite our Blessed Mother to join us on this journey as we pray to be blessed by her wisdom and grace.

Let us end where we began, and let us begin where we have ended.

Take a few moments to consider your prayer life. The Rosary and the mysteries of the faith contained within it can spark your conversation with God each day or deepen it. Answer this challenge, not just for yourself but for your family and your loved ones. In the process, you will discover the real you: the soul God blesses and called to serve him with love in this world.

Try it. Just pray it.

MORE ABOUT REAL MEN PRAY THE ROSARY, INC.

Real Men Pray the Rosary, Inc. (RMPTR) is an apostolate that attempts to accept the call of Pope John Paul II to "promote the Rosary with conviction."

RMPTR was founded by us, David and Valerie Calvillo, on the Feast of the Annunciation on March 25, 2009, with a stated mission to *"rediscover the Rosary . . . in the light of Scripture, in harmony with the Liturgy, and in the context of our daily lives."* The language of our mission statement is taken directly from Pope John Paul II's Apostolic Letter *Rosarium Virginis Mariae.*

Education

One of RMPTR's primary objectives is to educate, especially using the "light of Scripture" as a starting point. RMPTR has undertaken to educate Catholics and non-Catholics alike about the Rosary. RMPTR maintains an active website at realmen praytherosary.org. We have published educational materials that explain how to pray the Rosary and that underscore the beauty underlying the Mysteries comprising the core of the Rosary prayer.

Evangelization

The educational aspect of our work also shows up in evangelization efforts. RMPTR's Facebook page has exploded during its short life, building a community of people from throughout the world who follow the daily Rosary Mystery reflections offered by RMPTR "in the context of our daily lives." Many in the community interact and add their own reflections, intentions, and teachings. The online community—about half from the United States and the other half from almost every Christian nation in the world—prays together and joins together on this social media site. RMPTR also sells its evangelization products, or "gear," in the United States and in several other countries: T-shirts, caps, coffee mugs, and more. These evangelization efforts also take the form of speaking engagements. Valerie and I have been invited to speak at several events, including men's conferences, retreats, Confirmation classes, and similar gatherings.

Fostering Prayer in Our Community

As a direct result of an inspirational late-night visit to the website www.rosaryarmy.com, I, the world's most clumsy former Boy Scout, learned to tie Rosary knots. Valerie, of course, instantly perfected the technique. Locally, RMPTR has hosted RMPTR Rosary Tyings, where we gather as a community to make all-twine knotted Rosaries for ACTS retreats, Confirmation retreats, CCD classes, the troops in Iraq and Afghanistan, and sometimes simply to get together to pray. We tell folks that we'll gladly teach them how to make the Rosaries, but they have to promise to pass it on. In the same way that the Willits taught us how to make these Rosaries through their apostolate and website, we are passing this knowledge forward as well. These Rosary tyings bring the Body of Christ together to pray and to enjoy our common faith. It is certainly one of our favorite activities.

"Behold Your Mother"

As noted earlier in the book, my mom bequeathed to me a love for our Blessed Mother. Our love for Mary is thus an integral part of RMPTR—and of our marriage and family life. Because my conversion/reversion experience involved *The Secret of the Rosary* in a very direct way, I have since read almost everything that St. Louis de Montfort has written. These readings led me to the Total Consecration devotion and to propose that Valerie and

I consecrate our marriage to our Blessed Mother. We've since become involved in bringing together people in our Diocese of Brownsville, Texas, to undertake de Montfort's thirty-three-day preparation process and make the Act of Total Consecration.

Totus Tuus—John Paul II's papal motto, based on St. Louis de Montfort's spirituality—is very much a reality within RMPTR, and that directive weaves itself throughout the execution of our mission. RMPTR is one of many apostolates that try to spread the good news of the gospel and, in particular, to please Jesus Christ and his Mother by propagating the praying of the Most Holy Rosary of the Blessed Virgin Mary. We pray they are pleased with our little efforts.

Totus Tuus.

PAPAL AND MAGISTERIAL DOCUMENTS ON THE ROSARY

These Encyclical Letters by Popes Leo XIII, Pius XII, and Paul VI, highlight the prominent place the Rosary has held in the papal teachings for hundreds of years. These three happen to be some of the most pertinent and directed of papal documents that deal with the Rosary and its place in our spiritual lives as Catholics and Christian men. The versions below have been shortened and adapted. More complete materials can be found on our website realmenpraytherosary.org.

I have found it worth reading through these letters several times, along with other papal writings on the Rosary, and reflecting on the many insights and fatherly advice the popes offer to us. I recommend you make this a part of your spiritual reading program, too. There is so much you can learn from these wise men who led the Church in times as perilous and uncertain as our own.

The additional meditation by Cardinal Alfonso López Trujillo —president of the Pontifical Council for the Family—on the Rosary as a *family* prayer speaks directly to the purpose of this book: how and why we, as men, must incorporate prayer— especially this prayer—into our lives as husbands and fathers. This document is also worthy of some time and consideration as you contemplate exactly what role the prayer of the Rosary will play in your life.

Excerpts from Fidentem Piumque Animum Encyclical of Pope Leo XIII on the Most Holy Rosary[1]

We can never be satisfied with celebrating the Divine Mother, who is in truth worthy of all praise, and in urging love and affection towards her who is also the mother of mankind, who is *full of mercy, full of grace.*

Everyone who prays finds the door open to impetration, both from the very nature of prayer and from the promises of Christ. And we all know that prayer derives its chief efficacy from two principal circumstances: perseverance, and the union of many for one end. The former is signified in those invitations of Christ so full of goodness: *ask, seek, knock* (Mt 7:7), just as a kind father desires to indulge the wishes of his children, but who also requires to be continually asked by them and as it were wearied by their prayers, in order to attach their hearts more closely to himself. The second condition our Lord has born witness to more than once: *If two of you shall consent upon earth concerning anything whatsoever they shall ask, it shall be done to them by My Father who is in heaven. For where there are two or three gathered in My name, there am I in the midst of them* (Mt 18:19, 20). Both of these qualities are conspicuous in the Rosary. For, to be brief, by repeating the same prayers we strenuously implore from our Heavenly Father the Kingdom of His grace and glory; we again and again beseech the Virgin Mother to aid us sinners by her prayers, both during our whole life and especially at that last moment which is the stepping-stone to eternity. The formula of the Rosary, too, is excellently adapted to prayer in common, so that it has been styled, not without reason, "The Psalter of Mary." And that old custom of our forefathers ought to be preserved or else restored, according to which Christian families, whether in town or country, were religiously wont at close of day, when their labors were at an end, to assemble before a figure of Our Lady and alternately recite the Rosary. She, delighted at this faithful and unanimous homage, was ever near them like a loving mother surrounded by her children, distributing to them the blessings of domestic peace, the foretaste of the peace of heaven.

Another excellent fruit follows from the Rosary, exceedingly opportune to the character of our times. This we have referred to elsewhere. It is that, whilst the virtue of Divine Faith is daily exposed to so many dangers and attacks, the Christian may here derive nourishment and strength for his faith. . . . All know the value and merit of faith. For faith is just like a most precious gem, producing now the blossoms of all virtue by which we are pleasing to God, and hereafter to bring forth fruits that will last forever: *for to know Thee is perfect justice, and to know Thy justice and Thy power is the root of immortality.* . . . To those therefore who are striving after supreme happiness this means of the Rosary has been most providentially offered, and it is one unsurpassed for facility and convenience. The example of Christ is before us, for in order that His disciples *might be one* in faith and charity, he poured forth prayer and supplication to His Father. And concerning the efficacious prayer of His most holy Mother for the same end, there is a striking testimony in the Acts of the Apostles. Therein is described the first assembly of the Disciples, expecting with earnest hope and prayer the promised fullness of the Holy Spirit. And the presence of Mary united with them in prayer is specially indicated: *All these were persevering with one mind in prayer with Mary the Mother of Jesus.*

Excerpts from Ingruentium Malorum *Encyclical of Pope Pius XII on Reciting the Rosary*[2]

Mindful of that Divine teaching: "Ask and it shall be given to you; seek and you shall find; knock, and it shall be opened to you" (Lk 11:9), fly with confidence to the Mother of God. There, the Christian people have always sought chief refuge in the hour of danger, because "she has been constituted the cause of salvation for the whole human race" (St. Irenaeus).

We well know the Rosary's powerful efficacy to obtain the maternal aid of the Virgin. By no means is there only one way to pray to obtain this aid. However, We consider the Holy Rosary the most convenient and most fruitful means, as is clearly suggested by the very origin of this practice, heavenly rather than human, and by its nature. What prayers are better adapted and more beautiful than the Lord's prayer and the angelic salutation, which are the flowers with which this mystical crown is formed? With meditation of the Sacred Mysteries added to the vocal prayers, there emerges another very great advantage, so that all, even the most simple and least educated, have in this a prompt and easy way to nourish and preserve their own faith.

And truly, from the frequent meditation on the Mysteries, the soul little by little and imperceptibly draws and absorbs the virtues they contain, and is wondrously enkindled with a longing for things immortal, and becomes strongly and easily impelled to follow the path which Christ Himself and His Mother have followed. The recitation of identical formulas repeated so many times, rather than rendering the prayer sterile and boring, has on the contrary the admirable quality of infusing confidence in him who prays and brings to bear a gentle compulsion on the motherly Heart of Mary.

But it is above all in the bosom of the family that We desire the custom of the Holy Rosary to be everywhere adopted, religiously preserved, and ever more intensely practiced. What a sweet sight—most pleasing to God—when, at eventide, the Christian home resounds with the frequent repetition of praises in honor of the august Queen of Heaven! It links all more tightly in a sweet bond of love, with the most Holy Virgin, who, like a loving mother, in the circle of her children, will be there bestowing upon them an abundance of the gifts of concord and family peace.

Then the home of the Christian family, like that of Naza-reth, will become an earthly abode of sanctity, and, so to speak, a sacred temple, where the Holy Rosary will not only be the particular prayer which every day rises to heaven in an odor of sweetness, but will also form the most efficacious school of Christian discipline and Christian virtue.

Excerpts from Christi Matri
Encyclical of Pope Paul VI on Prayers for Peace during October[3]

It is a solemn custom of the faithful during the month of October to weave the prayers of the Rosary into mystical garlands for the Mother of Christ. Following in the footsteps of our predecessors, We heartily approve this, and We call upon all the sons of the church to offer special devotions to the Most Blessed Virgin this year. For the danger of a more serious and extensive calamity hangs over the human family and has increased, especially in parts of eastern Asia where a bloody and hard-fought war is rag-ing. So We feel most urgently that We must once again do what We can to safeguard peace. We are also disturbed by what We know to be going on in other areas, such as the growing nuclear armaments race, the senseless nationalism, the racism, the obses-sion for revolution, the separations imposed upon citizens, the nefarious plots, the slaughter of innocent people. All of these can furnish material for the greatest calamity.

If evils increase, the devotion of the People of God should also increase. And so, venerable brothers, We want you to take the lead in urging and encouraging people to pray ardently to our most merciful mother Mary by saying the Rosary during the month of October, as We have already indicated. This prayer is well-suited to the devotion of the People of God, most pleasing to the Mother of God and most effective in gaining heaven's blessings.

This very fruitful way of praying is not only efficacious in warding off evils and preventing calamities, but is also of great help in fostering Christian life. "It nourishes the Catholic faith which readily takes on new life from a timely commentary on the sacred mysteries, and it turns minds toward the truths that have been taught us by God."

Excerpts from The Rosary as Family Prayer by Cardinal Alfonso López Trujillo[4]

We know well how deeply rooted Marian devotion is in the heart of Peter's Successor. He placed his ministry under her protection, *"Totus tuus,"* and we know that the Rosary has a special place in his devotions. We are used to seeing him with the Rosary beads between his fingers. His desire is for the Rosary to become popular again, especially in families.

The Rosary, in its simplicity and depth, goes to the heart of Christian experience in the dialogue of faith expressed in prayer. It has a strong evangelizing impact. The members of the family can contemplate the central events at the heart of the faith through the mysteries. Now, we have the mysteries of light, in which we are invited to reflect on the wedding of Cana and on the beginning of a new family. We could say that in the Our Father and Hail Mary, we find a synthesis in which a dynamic, effective transmission of the faith passes through it that fortifies the experience of the family community in a special union that is a powerful aid because it is also stable and solid before the Lord of the Covenant.

As the Holy Father says in *Familiaris Consortio*: "only by praying together with their children can a father and mother—exercising their royal priesthood—penetrate the innermost depths of their children's hearts and leave an impression that the future events in their lives will not be able to efface" (n. 60).

One writer said that in the evangelized nations in every family, at nightfall, the recitation of the Rosary rose like a symphony.

Why should we not strive to restore this witness, imbuing the domestic church with the Word that all may savor, sharing it with children like bread, in an attitude that will evangelize a society that is in danger of growing cold and falling away from God?

NOTES

Chapter 1. The Rosary for Our Times

1. *Angelus*, October 29, 1978.

2. Please visit our website at www.realmenpraytherosary.org for a list of CDs, DVDs, and audio files that we've found useful.

Chapter 2. A Prayer for Men

1. St. Louis de Montfort. *Treatise on True Devotion to Jesus through Mary*, n. 59.

Chapter 3. A History of the Rosary

1. *Catholic Encyclopedia*, "Rosary," I.

2. Ibid.

3. Augusta Theodosia Drane, *The History of St. Dominic, Founder of the Friars Preachers* (New York: Longmans, Green and Co., 1891), 122.

4. Cited in P. Denys Mézard, O.P., *Etude sur les origines du Rosaire* (Rhône, 1912), 414–15.

5. Calvary de Pontchâteau, "History of the Calvary," http://www.calvairedepontchateau.com/calvary/history, accessed November 20, 2012.

Chapter 4. How to Pray the Rosary: The Prayers

1. St. Alphonsus di Liguori. *Glories of Mary* (New York: Benziger Brothers, 1902), 167.

Chapter 6. Real Men Pray for Women

1. St. Louis de Montfort. *Treatise on True Devotion to Jesus through Mary*, n. 108.

2. Ibid., n. 157.

3. Ibid., n. 108.

Appendix B. Papal and Magisterial Documents on the Rosary

1. Full text available at http://www.vatican.va/holy_father/leo_xiii/encyclicals/documents/hf_l-xiii_enc_20091896_fidentem-piumque-animum_en.html.

2. Full text available at www.vatican.va/holy_father/pius_xii/encyclicals/documents/hf_p-xii_enc_15091951_ingruentium-malorum_en.html.

3. Full text available at http://www.vatican.va/holy_father/paul_vi/encyclicals/documents/f_p-vi_enc_15091966_christi-matri_en.html.

4. Full text available at: http://www.vatican.va/roman_curia/pontifical_councils/family/documents/rc_pc_family_doc_20030204_rosary-trujillo_en.html.

David N. Calvillo, a former adjunct law and university professor, is now a practicing civil trial lawyer and bilingual mediator with the Calvillo Law Firm. After a profound spiritual experience praying the Rosary while on retreat, Calvillo and his wife Valerie founded Real Men Pray the Rosary, launching a global movement of prayer and devotion. Calvillo is a fourth degree Knight of Columbus and has served his parishes on pastoral and finance councils and as eucharistic minister and lector. Calvillo formerly served in leadership of his diocesan chapter of ACTS Catholic retreats and remains active in the organization. He served his community as president of the Boys and Girls Club of McAllen and lives in southern Texas with his wife and their seven children.

Founded in 1865, Ave Maria Press,
a ministry of the Congregation of
Holy Cross, is a Catholic publishing
company that serves the spiritual and
formative needs of the Church and its
schools, institutions, and ministers;
Christian individuals and families; and
others seeking spiritual nourishment.

For a complete listing of titles from

Ave Maria Press

Sorin Books

Forest of Peace

Christian Classics

visit www.avemariapress.com

ave maria press® / Notre Dame, IN 46556
A Ministry of the United States Province of Holy Cross